ONCE SAVED, ALWAYS SAVED?

A Free Grace Defense

Edited by
Shawn Lazar

Contributors:
Aaron Aquinas, Charles C. Bing, L. E. Brown, Marty Cauley, Sarah Coleman, Antonio da Rosa, Daniel Goepfrich, Eli Haitov, Grant Hawley, Marcia Hornok, Lucas Kitchen, Valtteri Lahti, Dominick Macelli, Kenneth McClure, Jeremy Mikkelsen, Chris Morrison, Luke Morrison, Tim Nichols, Nate Otto, Allen Rea, Vincenzo Russo, Summer Stevens, Jon Tretsven, Daniel Weierbach, Shawn Willson

Longview, TX

Once Saved, Always Saved? A Free Grace Defense © 2025 by Free Grace International

Published by Free Grace International
2 Circle Rd
Longview, TX 75602
www.freegrace.in

ISBN: 978-1-68543-034-4 (Paperback)
　　　978-1-68543-035-1 (Kindle)

All rights reserved. Any part of this publication may be reproduced, stored in a retrieval system, or transmitted in any form or by any means—electronic, mechanical, photocopying, recording, or otherwise.

The publisher grants permission to distribute this work freely, provided it is not sold and its wording remains unchanged.

Contents

Introduction: You Can't Lose What You Didn't Earn 7
Shawn Lazar

Section 1: Core Concepts

What Is "Free Grace Theology"? 21
Charles C. Bing

Eternal Rewards: An Introduction 25
Lucas Kitchen

Eternal Security and the Early Church 31
Valtteri Lahti

Section 2: Key Passages

1 Corinthians 9:24-27 41
Luke Morrison

Romans 11 45
Tim Nichols

Hebrews 6:4–9 49
Daniel Goepfrich

Hebrews 10:26-31 55
Jeremy Mikkelsen

2 Peter 2:20-22 63
Eli Haitov

James 5:19-20 67
Shawn Willson

So What Is "Salvation" in James? 73
    Chris Morrison

Matthew 24:13 83
    Daniel Weierbach

Revelation 3:5 87
    Luke Morrison

The Book of Life and Revelation 3:5 91
    Marty Cauley

Ephesians 1:13-14 95
    Kenneth McClure

A Dual Seal in Ephesians 1:13-14 99
    Marty Cauley

Romans 7 103
    L. E. Brown

Romans 8:29-30 107
    Marty Cauley

Section 3: More Reasons

Sola Fide: Professed by Most, Truly Believed by Few 113
    Vincenzo Russo

Can You Lose Your Salvation? 123
    Jon Tretsven

A Response to "Whoever Believes" as Present Tense 129
    Aaron Aquinas

You Are Saved "If" (Colossians 1:23) 137
    Nate Otto

Carnal Christians: No Such Thing? 141
    Grant Hawley

Is Grace a License to Sin? 147
    Lucas Kitchen

Grace Is Not a License to Sin 151
    Antonio da Rosa

The Rich Beggar 157
   Marcia Hornok

Parents: Let the Doctrine of Eternal Security Bring You Peace 159
   Summer Stevens

Why Eternal Security Is Important to Me 163
   Dominick Macelli

Suicide Is My Story, Assurance Is My Song 167
   Sarah Coleman

How Eternal Security Encourages Missionaries 171
   Allen Rea

Subject Index 175

Scripture Index 177

Contributing Authors 185

Introduction: You Can't Lose What You Didn't Earn

SHAWN LAZAR

"Once saved, always saved flies in the face of the constant teaching of the Bible, from Genesis 1 to Revelation's end." ~Scot McKnight

Introduction

You're probably reading this book because you've seen *Once Saved, Always Saved? A Documentary Film*. Put simply, the documentary denies the doctrine of eternal security. The speakers effectively claim that salvation is like holding a greased watermelon in a bathtub—slip up, and you'll lose it!

Well, I've got good news for you—they're wrong. Eternal security is true. The authors in this book all believe in the doctrine of "once saved, always saved," not because of wishful thinking, laziness, or a desire to live however we want, but because the Bible teaches it. That's what Free Grace theology holds to, and what this book will defend.

Outrageous Grace

Are we secure forever, no matter what? That might sound outrageous and unfair. But that's the point. The Gospel isn't about what's fair. The Gospel is about "grace upon grace" (John 1:16 ESV).

If you find eternal security hard to believe, I'd agree with you—*if we were talking about anything other than salvation*. If something sounds "too good to be true," it probably is. However, the Gospel is the big exception. It's over-the-top good news!

In this Introduction, I aim to cover four Free Grace basics so that readers can better understand the theological terrain before delving into the details of specific problem passages raised by the documentary. First, I'll present five differences between eternal security and perseverance of the saints. Second, I will present fifteen reasons to believe in eternal security. Third, I will discuss whether the documentary teaches the concept of works salvation.

Eternal Security and Perseverance Are Different Doctrines

From a Free Grace perspective, there is a fundamental confusion at the heart of the documentary. The speakers conflate distinct doctrines: the perseverance of the saints (hereafter POTS) and eternal security, also known as once saved, always saved (hereafter OSAS). Those concepts have been used interchangeably in the past, but they shouldn't be, since they represent different beliefs. For example, Matthew Pinson states, "The patristic fathers did not believe in once saved, always saved. They believed there was a possibility of turning from Christ. And so they would have a position much like modern Arminians on the possibility of apostasy." In his estimation, OSAS is incompatible with apostasy. In fact, the speakers in the documentary spend much of their time demonstrating that believers can stray from the faith, thinking that this disproves OSAS. But that's a mistake. Eternal security is compatible with Christians falling away from the faith.

Here are five differences between POTS and OSAS.

First, POTS and OSAS belong to different theological traditions. While POTS is part of Augustinianism, Calvinism, and Reformed thought, OSAS is not (at least, not necessarily). Many OSAS advocates identify with Baptist Traditionalism, Provisionism, and Free Grace theology.

Second, POTS and OSAS have different foundations. Whereas POTS is founded on (the Calvinist) doctrine of unconditional election, OSAS is based on biblical promises that salvation is irrevocable.[1]

---

[1] Incidentally, many of us in the Free Grace movement believe in election to service, not to eternal life. See my book *Chosen to Serve* for a defense of the idea that election is to service, not to eternal life.

Third, POTS and OSAS have different views of how to be saved. Although both theologies claim to believe in salvation by faith, POTS advocates typically teach that you are born again or justified by a continuous faith that produces good works, which is a "gift" that God only gives to the elect, so that if someone falls away from the faith or commits a grave sin, that proves they were never saved to begin with. For them, salvation depends not only on *what* you believe but also on *how* you believe it—i.e., it must be with persevering "gift" faith. By contrast, OSAS says salvation requires a single act of faith in Jesus. The moment you believe in Him, you have everlasting life and are secure forever. Continuous faith and works are essential for discipleship and spiritual growth, not salvation.

Fourth, POTS and OSAS take different perspectives on the concept of sanctification. According to POTS, sanctification is unconditional. God causes the elect to be sanctified and guarantees they will never fall into major sin or apostasy in this life but will persevere in faith and good works until death. By contrast, OSAS sees sanctification as conditional. You must choose to be a doer of the word, build your life on the solid rock, and make every effort to add goodness, knowledge, self-control, and other virtues to grow to spiritual maturity in faith (cf. Matt 7:24; Jas 1:22; 2 Pet 1:5-6). Growth is not automatic. Believers have free will. Instead of choosing faithfulness, a believer can choose to backslide, remain carnal, or even apostatize. But they remain eternally secure.

Fifth, POTS and OSAS have different effects on assurance. Under POTS, you shouldn't be sure of your salvation because you can't know if you're one of the elect or that you'll persevere. If you can't be sure that you won't apostatize in the future, then you can't be sure that you're saved now. (By the way, that same criticism applies to the speakers in the documentary. They can't have assurance either.) By contrast, under OSAS, you can be assured of your salvation, because it is based on the truthfulness of Jesus' promise, not on our behavior.

I hope you see that POTS and OSAS are two different doctrines. Although the speakers in the documentary confuse the two, attacking elements of both, this book focuses on defending OSAS or eternal security.

However, that raises the question: Are there any Biblical reasons to believe in eternal security?

Fifteen Reasons for Eternal Security

The documentary claims that eternal security "flies in the face of the constant teaching of the Bible from Genesis 1 to Revelation's end." If they mean POTS flies in the face of the Bible, then I would agree. But eternal security is strongly implied by Scripture. Indeed, here are thirteen Biblical reasons why eternal security is true.

First, salvation is by grace. "For it is by grace you have been saved..." (Eph 2:8). Grace means you didn't earn salvation and can't lose it. On the contrary, you deserve death and condemnation, not salvation. "If you, LORD, kept a record of sins, Lord, who could stand?" (Ps 130:3). The answer is no one. Therefore, no one could earn salvation by being good. That's why God, in His sovereignty and mercy, decided to save people irrespective of what they deserved. If grace excludes *merit* as a ground for *earning* it, it also excludes *demerit* as a ground for *losing* it. Thus, there's no logical or moral basis for Him to revoke it later due to undeserving behavior such as apostasy. What grace gives, performance can't cancel.

Second, salvation is through faith. The one condition of salvation is to believe in Jesus. It's that simple. "Yet to all who did receive him, to those who *believed in his name*, he gave the right to become children of God" (John 1:12, emphasis added). "For God so loved the world that he gave his one and only Son, that whoever *believes in him* shall not perish but have eternal life" (John 3:16, emphasis added). "*Believe in the Lord Jesus*, and you will be saved—you and your household." (Acts 16:31, emphasis added). No works are required for salvation because salvation isn't a competition where God intends to exclude as many people as possible, but an invitation to save as many as possible. In His grace, God made salvation as *easy* as possible, requiring a single act of faith in Jesus. The Lord compared saving faith to how the Israelites looked at the bronze serpent and were healed. They didn't have to keep looking until the end of their lives to be healed. It only took a single look (cf. John 3:14). Likewise, one look at the Son—one act of faith—and you'll be saved forever (cf. John 3:15-18). Saving faith is often described as occurring in a decisive moment (using the aorist tense, e.g., Acts 4:4; Rom 4:3; Gal

3:6; Rom 10:9; Eph 1:13). While Scripture exhorts us to continue in the faith for the purpose of spiritual maturity and eternal rewards, the initial moment of faith is portrayed as sufficient to secure salvation.

Third, salvation is given apart from your works. You could never earn your salvation. Your best day wouldn't be good enough. That's why God could only give salvation apart from your works. It's "not by works, so that no one can boast" (Eph 2:9). "He saved us, not because of righteous things we had done, but because of his mercy" (Titus 3:5a). Salvation was never based on behavior: "Now to the one who works, wages are not credited as a gift but as an obligation. However, to the one who does not work but trusts God who justifies the ungodly, their faith is credited as righteousness" (Rom 4:4-5). If salvation didn't start with your works, it can't be taken away by your failures.

Fourth, salvation is a gift. Your good works can earn rewards in heaven, but they can't earn salvation (cf. 1 Cor 3:11-15). While the penalty of death is paid like a wage, eternal life is given freely as a gift: "For the wages of sin is death, but the gift of God is eternal life in Christ Jesus our Lord" (Rom 6:23). As Paul famously told the Ephesians, "For it is by grace you have been saved, through faith—and this is not from yourselves, it is the gift of God—not by works, so that no one can boast" (Eph 2:8-9). And when God gives you a gift, He does not take it back. Paul specifically affirmed the principle that "God's gifts and his call are irrevocable" (Rom 11:29). In other words, once God gives you the gift of salvation, He will never take it back. You have it forever.

Fifth, believers are already justified. A Judgment Day is coming and Jesus has been appointed Judge: "He commanded us to preach to the people and to testify that he is the one whom God appointed as judge of the living and the dead" (Acts 10:42); "For he has set a day when he will judge the world with justice by the man he has appointed. He has given proof of this to everyone by raising him from the dead" (Acts 17:31); "Moreover, the Father judges no one, but has entrusted all judgment to the Son" (John 5:22). Jesus will judge our every thought, word, and deed. The good news is that the Judge has decided that if you believe in Him, you receive your verdict beforehand. He won't judge or condemn believers (cf. John 3:18; 5:24). Instead, they have already been reckoned righteous and justified. "Therefore, since we have been justified through faith, we have peace with God" (Rom 5:1). The point is, unlike in Arminianism, justification isn't a type of probation. God doesn't save you on a trial basis. It's a once-for-all declaration of righteousness. The sins you might commit in the future, which the omniscient God already knows about, don't negate your justified state now. The gavel has already come down: "Not guilty!" That's a permanent decision.

Sixth, believers are already forgiven. All the sins of the world—past, present, and future—were imputed to Jesus (cf. Isa 53:5-6; John 1:29). The Lord made that *provision* for everyone in the world (cf. 1 John 2:2), but the *application* comes when one has faith in Jesus. The moment you believe in Jesus, you're forgiven—*for all of it*. Paul explained that forgiveness and justification are two sides of the same coin. "David says the same thing when he speaks of the blessedness of the one to whom God credits righteousness apart from works: 'Blessed are those whose transgressions are forgiven, whose sins are covered. Blessed is the one whose sin the Lord will never count against them'" (Rom 4:6-8). When you believe in Jesus, God will never count your sins against you. As he wrote to the Colossians, "He forgave us *all* our sins" (Col 2:13, emphasis added; cf. Acts 13:38-39). True, God will *discipline* you for your sins, because He wants you to be free of their power and influence (cf. Heb 12:4-12). But you are completely forgiven. This strongly implies eternal security, because whatever sins you might think deserve losing your salvation have already been forgiven. God will never count them against you, because He's already counted them against Jesus.

Seventh, Jesus will not cast you out. People who deny eternal security think that God will do the very thing Jesus promised never to do: "All those the Father gives me will come to me, and whoever comes to me I will never drive away" (John 6:37). You might deserve to be cast out, but He won't do it. Some think Jesus is only referring to how He won't turn away anyone who believes in Him. That's also true. However, the context primarily focuses on the resurrection (vv 38-40). Come to Him once, and He guarantees you'll be raised in the end. His welcome isn't provisional, it's permanent.

Eighth, Jesus will never lose you. Jesus is the Good Shepherd and will never lose a single sheep. He made that promise knowing that sheep are prone to wander. Nevertheless, He promises never to lose you: "This is the will of him who sent me, that I shall lose none of all those he has given me..." (John 6:39). If you could lose your salvation due to apostasy, that would negate His promise. You're safe and secure, no matter how prone to lostness you may be. Your security rests on His success, not yours.

Ninth, no one can snatch you from His hand. When you believe in Jesus, you're safe in His and Father's hands. "My sheep listen to my voice; I know them, and they follow me. I give them eternal life, and they shall never perish; no one will snatch them out of my hand. My Father, who has given them to me, is greater than all; no one can snatch them out of my Father's hand. I and the Father are one" (John 10:27-30). Some people sophistically reply that we can still choose to jump out of His hand, but Jesus doesn't qualify His promise like that. You're in His and the Father's hands, and no one, not even you, can break their grip.

Tenth, God keeps you by His power. The Lord's power saves you, and He's promised to keep you safe: "This inheritance is kept in heaven for you, who through faith are shielded by God's power until the coming of the salvation that is ready to be revealed in the last time" (1 Pet 1:4-5). If salvation depended on your performance, you'd already be lost. But the good news is you're not holding onto God—He's holding onto you, and He promises to shield you until the end.

Eleventh, the Holy Spirit has sealed you. When you believed in Jesus, God sealed you with the Holy Spirit: "When you believed, you were marked in him with a seal, the promised Holy Spirit, who is a deposit guaranteeing our inheritance until the redemption of those who are God's possession—to the praise of his glory" (Eph 1:13-14). You're sealed until the day of redemption: "And do not grieve the Holy Spirit of God, with whom you were sealed for the day of redemption" (Eph 4:30). You can grieve the Spirit, but that doesn't unseal you. His mark is permanent.

Twelfth, God finishes what He starts. Some people think that salvation begins by grace, but it's up to you to finish the job. But salvation isn't your project—it's God's. And Paul clarifies that "he who began a good work in you will carry it on to completion until the day of Christ Jesus" (Phil 1:6). If you could lose your salvation, Paul couldn't be confident that God would finish what He started. But since God does finish what He starts, once you're saved, you'll always be saved.

Thirteenth, nothing can separate you from God's love. There's not a power in the universe that can cut you off from God's love in Christ. "For I am convinced that neither death nor life, neither angels nor demons, neither the present nor the future, nor any powers, neither height nor depth, nor anything else in all creation, will be able to separate us from the love of God that is in Christ Jesus our Lord" (Rom 8:38-39). Romans 8 begins with the promise that whoever is in Christ will not be condemned (cf. Rom 8:1). The entire chapter presents a case for God's unbreakable commitment to the believer. And here we're told, in absolute terms, that no created power, whether death, or demons, or the future, can separate us from God's love. You're safe forever.

Fourteenth, He is faithful even when you are faithless. As Paul told Timothy, "if we are faithless, he remains faithful, for he cannot disown himself" (2 Tim 2:13). That whole passage is enlightening. It's about enduring in the faith to reign with Christ (one of many eternal rewards). If you don't endure—if you end up being an unworthy or unfaithful servant—then you'll be denied the right to reign. But you won't lose your salvation. Even if you're faithless to Him, He'll remain faithful to you. That's what He's promised, and He will not deny His own promises.

Fifteenth, Scripture never says you can lose your salvation. Not once. Yes, there are many warning passages in Scripture, but a careful reading of them will show they don't concern losing your eternal salvation. A believer who rebels against God has a lot to lose, but salvation isn't one of those things, as the other authors in this volume will explain. I know this is an argument from silence, but I would expect such a significant possibility to be taught clearly in Scripture.

There you have a case for eternal security in a nutshell. The other authors in this book will present their own arguments and properly explain verses that are often misinterpreted as contradicting the eternal security of the believer.

Does the Documentary Teach Works Salvation?

When people think that salvation depends on perseverance, they usually affirm some form of works salvation—if only inconsistently. From a Free Grace perspective, it was gratifying to hear the documentary speakers affirm salvation by grace, through faith, apart from works. I was also happy to hear them deny that they believe in salvation by works; however, they are inconsistent.

For example, in an interview for the documentary (although not included in the documentary itself), Pastor Joe Schimmel was asked, "Do you believe in a works-based salvation?" People who had watched the documentary received the impression that he did. He answered, "Absolutely not. In fact, if you're trying to be saved through doing a bunch of good works, that's actually one of the ways you can forfeit salvation." I strongly agree with him that works salvation is a false gospel. Every author in this book would agree.

While I hope that Schimmel actually believes that works salvation is wrong, at the beginning of the documentary, Schimmel faults the doctrine of eternal security for creating hypocrites who do not live holy lives, which he implies is necessary to be saved: "I believe it's a lot of the explanation of the hypocrisy in the American church and much of the church around the world today because there's a lot of people that are living like hypocrites because they've been taught that they don't have to live holy lives. I mean, we're talking about heaven and hell—we're talking about, eternal life." According to Schimmel, why is living a holy life important? Apparently, because salvation is not by faith apart from works. For Schimmel, salvation evidently depends on living a holy life. Otherwise, if you are a hypocrite, you will go to hell. He confirms this impression later in the documentary when he says: "People are taught that once you're saved, you can rebel against God, and you can live like hell and still enter the kingdom of heaven. That is a lie from the pit of hell." In other words, for him, entering the kingdom of heaven depends on not rebelling against God or engaging in too much sin. That clearly means salvation depends on our behavior, i.e., works salvation. Free Grace rejects such confusion.

People are never perfectly rational. We often hold contradictory beliefs, stating one thing is true, and then immediately affirming a conflicting belief. I think that kind of cognitive dissonance is evident in the documentary. It seemed clear to me, as it does to many people who have watched it, that the speakers believe that salvation is gained or lost depending on one's behavior. For example, Ben Witherington says, "It's not over till it's over. No Christian life should be judged in advance." In other words, no Christian life can be judged to be saved in advance of the Last Judgment, because salvation depends on how we lived our whole life, i.e., it will depend upon our works. He goes on to summarize the beliefs of the early church with evident approval, saying, "There wasn't some kind of airtight guarantee of salvation, regardless of your belief or behavior." In other words, for the early church, as for Witherington, salvation is not guaranteed apart from our behavior. But how can salvation depend on behavior if it's not based on works?

Likewise, Michael Brown says, "If we lean on his grace, and don't willfully play games with sin, we have nothing to fear. If we choose to play games with sin, we have everything to fear." The fear in question is one of losing salvation. Thus, for Brown, staying saved requires changing one's behavior and not "playing games with sin." In other words, salvation depends upon our works.

Similarly, Scot McKnight says about the early church: "They had inherited a Bible that taught people to believe, to obey. They knew no other way in the early church than faithfulness over the long haul." He makes that point against eternal security because, for McKnight, salvation evidently depends, not just on faith, but on faithfulness over the long haul.

Jessie Morrell is an example of this cognitive dissonance and confusion: "If we're justified by faith, which is a living faith that results in works, it's not works that justifies us. Works are just the evidence of God—of living faith. And as long as we are in the faith and we have the faith, then we have the promises of faith, like eternal life and the forgiveness of sin." On the surface, Morrell's comment looks like an affirmation of salvation by faith. But notice that he says one is only saved by having a "living faith," which he defines as one that results in doing good works. If one doesn't do good works, they don't have a living faith and can't be saved. This is verbal sleight-of-hand that introduces works into the condition of salvation by redefining faith to include them. Imagine if I claim that a gym membership is free but then say that a "living membership" will pay $50 a month, otherwise you'll forfeit the membership. Is that gym free? Absolutely not. In Free Grace circles, this is referred to as "backloading the gospel." How many good works must one do to have "living faith" enough to be saved by faith apart from works? Such confusion about salvation by faith alone is devastating.

This commitment to works-based salvation is also evident in how the speakers discuss repentance. They're clear that repentance is a condition of salvation. They're also clear that repentance includes a lifestyle change. For example, Sharon Johnson said, "Jesus preached repentance. He preached, 'Repent, change your mind, change your life.' If you don't change your mind, you can't change your life." For her, salvation depends on repentance, which involves changing one's life or behavior. Hence, for her, salvation must depend upon behavior (i.e., works).

I could go on, but please watch the documentary for yourself. I want to believe the speakers affirm salvation by grace, through faith, apart from works. However, they're living with the cognitive dissonance of also believing that salvation depends on changing one's lifestyle—especially that it depends upon avoiding major sins and rebellion—making salvation depend on our works. Like most Arminians, they're confused, or at least deeply inconsistent, about justification by faith apart from works.

That's the principal thing that I love about Free Grace theology: it unambiguously and consistently holds to salvation by grace, through faith, apart from works—without gimmicks or fine print.

Unity Without Uniformity

As I mentioned earlier, each of the authors in this book adheres to what has become known as Free Grace theology.[2] While every contrib-

---

[2] There is a growing literature about Free Grace theology. Here is a sampling of classic and newer works to explore: *Freely By His Grace: Classical Free Grace Theology*, eds. J. B. Hixson, Rick Whitmire, and Roy B. Zuck (Duluth, MN: Grace Gospel Press, 2012); *21 Tough Questions about Grace*, ed. Grant Hawley (Allen, TX: Bold Grace Ministries, 2015); David R. Anderson, *Free Grace Soteriology*, Revised Edition, ed. James S. Reitman (N.P.: Grace Theology Press, 2012); Charles C. Bing, *Grace, Salvation & Discipleship: How to Understand Some Difficult Passages* (N.P.: Grace Theology Press, 2015); Zane C. Hodges, *Absolutely Free! A Biblical Reply to Lordship Salvation* (Grand Rapids, MI: Zondervan, 1989); Lucas Kitchen, *Eternal Clarity: Erase the Gray Between Believe and Obey* (Longview, TX: Free Grace International, 2021); Shawn Lazar, *The Five Points of Free Grace* (Longview, TX: Free Grace International, 2024); Charles Ryrie, *So Great Salvation: What It Means to Believe in Jesus Christ* (Wheaton, IL: Victor Books, 1989); Robert N. Wilkin, *Confident in Christ: Living By Faith Really Works* (Second Edition) (Denton, TX: Grace Evangelical Society, 1999, 2015).

utor to this volume affirms the core tenets of Free Grace theology, that unity does not require absolute unanimity on every interpretive point, theological nuance, or pastoral application. Readers should understand, then, that inclusion in this collection does not imply that every contributor agrees completely with every other. Just as the speakers in the documentary represent a spectrum of Arminianism, this book represents a spectrum of Free Grace theology. The diversity of thought represented here reflects the freedom of grace itself—freedom to think, study, and reason from Scripture without fear of being expelled for differences in non-essential matters. It also reflects the strength of the Free Grace position: that it can be robustly defended from multiple angles, by writers and pastors who may differ on many things but are united by the gospel of grace in Jesus Christ.

Conclusion

Salvation is the most important question one can settle in this life. Nothing else comes close. It's natural to wonder if something so precious can be lost. Is our eternal destiny hanging by a thread? Are we doomed always to wonder if we'll make it in the end?

The good news is that you can rest secure in Christ, not because of what you've done, but because of what He's promised.

Some people might think they're too far gone to be saved. If that's what you're thinking, let me remind you: you can't lose what you didn't earn. It's not about you. It's about Christ. He didn't come for the righteous. He came for the broken, the beaten up, and the bums. That means there's hope for you. Just stop looking at yourself and keep your eyes on Christ. He is faithful even to faithless people. That's His promise and guarantee.

There's much more to say about eternal security and how it fits into the larger picture of salvation, discipleship, and rewards. I'll leave that to the other authors in this volume to explain.

SECTION 1

Core Concepts

What Is "Free Grace Theology"?[1]

Charles C. Bing

Introduction

Theological labels are a convenient way to summarize belief systems. Many labels have become an established part of theological dialogue, like Arminianism, Calvinism, amillennialism, or premillennialism. Many who hear the label "Free Grace Theology" wonder what it means. Here is a brief summation.

    1. Free Grace teaches that the grace of salvation is absolutely free. This is the obvious place to begin, though it should be unnecessary to say this since the word grace (Greek *charis*) essentially means a free and undeserved gift. However, since some speak of costly or cheap grace, it is necessary to clarify that grace is totally free. That does not mean it is free to the giver, who in this case is God, but it means that no payment or merit is required from those to whom it is offered, which would be all unsaved and undeserving sinners. Romans 3:24 distinguishes between the free gift to the recipient and the cost to the Giver: "having been justified freely by His grace through the redemption that is in Christ Jesus."

    2. Free Grace means that the grace of salvation can be received only through faith. Since we as sinners can do nothing to earn God's grace, it has to be given as a gift which can only be received through faith. By faith (or believing, which is from the same Greek word) we mean

---

[1] Originally pubished as GraceNotes, no. 67. See https://www.gracelife.org/resources/gracenotes/?lang=eng&id=67

the human response of accepting something as true and trustworthy. It is a conviction, an inner persuasion. This definition precludes any other conditions of works, performance, or merit (Rom 4:4-5). Faith cannot be defined by obedience to Christian commands, baptism, surrender, commitment of one's life to God, or turning from sins. These things can and should be the results of faith, but they are distinct from faith itself, otherwise grace ceases to be grace (Rom 11:6). Ephesians 2:8 says, "For by grace you have been saved through faith, not by works…" Faith is a simple response, but that does not mean that it is an easy one. Many who hold to Free Grace believe that repentance, as a change of mind or heart, can sometimes be used to describe the aspect of faith in which we come to a conviction or persuasion about something. Other Free Grace proponents do not think repentance (as turning from sins) has any role in salvation or saving faith.

3. Free Grace believes the object of faith is the Lord Jesus Christ. Faith must always have an object, because faith itself is not the effective cause of our salvation (We are saved "by grace"), but the instrumental means through which we are saved ("through faith"). The One who actually saves us is the Lord Jesus Christ. But it is not any Jesus, it is Jesus as the Son of God who died for our sins and rose again and guarantees eternal salvation to all who believe in Him.

4. Free Grace holds to the finished work of Christ. Grace is free because Jesus Christ did all the work on our behalf. His proclamation "It is finished" on the cross means that He made the final and full payment for the penalty for our sins. It also means we cannot add anything to what Jesus accomplished. We cannot do anything to earn our salvation or to keep our salvation. Free Grace therefore teaches eternal security for the believer.

5. Free Grace provides the only basis for assurance of salvation. Any system or belief that requires our performance cannot give assurance of salvation. Human performance is subjective, variable, unpredictable, and always imperfect. Faith must rest in Jesus Christ and His promise as revealed in the Word of God. The person and work of Christ and the Word of God are objective truths that cannot change. Therefore Free Grace offers the only basis for full assurance of salvation.

6. Free Grace distinguishes between salvation and discipleship. While some theological systems believe that all Christians are disciples, Free Grace understands that the condition for eternal salvation (believe) is distinct from the many conditions for discipleship (deny oneself, take up your cross, follow Christ, abide in His Word, love Christ more than your family, etc.). Since grace is absolutely free, it cannot demand these conditions or it ceases to be grace. Free Grace believes that the commitments of discipleship should be the result of salvation, not the requirement. To make them conditions of salvation inserts works and human merit into the gospel of grace.

7. Free Grace teaches that the Christian life is also by grace through faith. Since we are saved by grace and kept saved by grace, we also grow by grace which is accessed through faith. Grace provides everything we don't deserve and more for anything we need. Just as in salvation, the grace to grow is available to us through faith: "through whom [the Lord Jesus Christ] also we have access by faith into this grace in which we stand. . ." (Rom 5:2; compare Gal 2:20).

8. Free Grace provides the best motivation for godly living. If salvation is by human performance, there is no assurance, and if there is no assurance, a motivation for good conduct easily becomes to prove we are saved or to avoid hell. Guilt, fear, and doubt can produce good conduct, but not necessarily godly conduct. Godly conduct includes the inner motivations of love and gratitude. The assurance of God's grace and the finished work of Christ allow Christians to grow in an environment of freedom and unconditional love (Titus 2:11-12).

9. Free Grace holds that the Christian is accountable. According to Free Grace, the believer is set free from any demands of the law or works as a basis for eternal salvation. But Free Grace also teaches that Christians should live godly lives because: 1) We should be grateful for what God has done (Rom 12:1-2); 2) God wants us to have good works (Eph 2:10); 3) We have a new position in Christ (Rom 6:1-14); 4) We have a new Master—Jesus (Rom 6:15-23); and 5) We have a new power—the Holy Spirit (Rom 8:1-11). Because of these things, Free Grace teaches that God will hold us accountable for the kind of lives we lead. God can discipline us in this life (Heb 12:5-11) and we will face the future Judgment Seat of Christ where believers will give an account to God (Rom 14:10-12; 1 Cor 3:11-4:5; 2 Cor 5:10). In this judgment, believers will be rewarded or denied rewards. In no way does Free Grace teach that Christians can sin without consequence.

10. Free Grace is committed first to an accurate interpretation of the Bible. This should go without saying, but is necessary because many have forced their theological systems on their interpretations instead of letting the Bible speak for itself. The Free Grace system is the result of a literal and plain sense approach to the Bible that considers God's various ways of administering His plan for the world through the ages, and the proper contexts of any Bible passage. The Free Grace system seeks above all to be biblical. Its first commitment is not to a theological system, but to what the Bible says, even if some particulars cannot be reconciled easily to other teachings or traditional interpretations. Therefore, the Free Grace position allows for various interpretations of some biblical passages as long as they are consistent with good principles of Bible interpretation and the clear teaching of God's free grace.

Conclusion

Free Grace theology begins with the plain and clear teaching of the Bible that grace is absolutely free. From this, the Bible's teachings about salvation, faith, security, assurance, the Christian life, and discipleship are viewed consistent with the unconditional nature of grace. The free grace of God should motivate Christians to worship, serve, and live godly for the "God of all grace" (1 Pet 5:10) who "first loved us" (1 John 4:19).

Eternal Rewards: An Introduction

Lucas Kitchen

"[Evangelical voices are saying] We might have our lives cut short as a result of sinful living. We might lose some of our heavenly reward. But no matter what we do, no matter how we live, we're still saved." ~Michael Brown

Introduction

This chapter, which is a summary of my book *Eternal Rewards: It Will Pay To Obey*, speaks to Christians about an incredible motivation we have available, and yet so few know about. The speakers in the documentary refer to heavenly rewards, but do not explain what they are. This article will show that eternal rewards are an integral part of New Testament teaching.

A Surprising Discovery

I grew up in a Bible teaching church, and I estimate I listened to over 10,000 talks on Biblical subjects. Yet those sermons almost never mentioned reward in Heaven as distinct from salvation. Only one sermon when I was in junior high whispered of rewards, and then the mystery was closed for years. Three decades of study gave me almost no awareness that there would be rewards above and beyond salvation for those who obey God.

In my early thirties, I began attending a church that taught on this topic. Skeptical at first, I assumed there were few Biblical references to reward. *How could I have missed something so fundamental?* I started researching. What I found shocked me: reference after reference to reward in Heaven. The concept appears under many terms, none of which means salvation. A simple thesis emerged: not everyone will be equal in Heaven; some Christians will gain reward for obedience, while others will miss out because of disobedience.

Jesus Himself taught this difference. In the Sermon on the Mount, He warned that "whoever breaks one of the least of these commands and teaches others to do the same will be called *least in the kingdom of heaven*. But whoever does and teaches these commands will be called *great in the kingdom of heaven*" (Matt 5:19, emphasis added). This clearly shows that not all believers will be equal in status in the kingdom of heaven. It's a shocking revelation, to be sure.

Curious how pervasive this idea was, I checked every New Testament book. I found direct references to eternal reward in 24 of the 27 books. The remaining three contain shorter references. I came to believe that every New Testament author speaks about eternal rewards. When they mention reward, they aren't describing salvation but *a bonus, extra payout, reimbursement in Heaven for work done on earth*. Believers are not forced to work for rewards; they are invited.

Reward Is Compensation

To reinforce this idea we must look at the original language. Several Greek words are translated as "reward." The most common are *misthos, antapodosis, misthapodosia*, and *apodidōmi*. None of these words means a free gift; they all mean a repayment for some action or work. Modern synonyms would be *wages, reimbursement, payment, and compensation*.

- *misthos*: used for wages owed for work; it never means a free gift.
- *antapodosis*: a compensating reward paid back for work or action.
- *misthapodosis*: recompense or repayment, whether positive or negative.
- *apodidōmi*: to pay what is owed.

Either way, the idea is the same: those who receive rewards in Heaven will get reimbursement for the work they've done. The work may not be easy, but that's why it will be worth it.

Gifts vs. Rewards

This distinction becomes clearer when Scripture compares gifts and rewards.

> **For the wages of sin is death, but the gift of God is eternal life… (Rom 6:23, emphasis added).**

Eternal isn't earned; it's a gift. Paul reminds us that we are saved by grace through faith, not by works (Eph 2:89). Eternal life, the Spirit's indwelling, and everlasting citizenship are *gifts*.

By contrast, believers are warned:

> **"Watch yourselves so that you don't lose what we have worked for, but that you may receive a full reward" (2 John 8, emphasis added).**

Similarly, Paul explains that each worker will receive his own reward according to his own labor. In 1 Corinthians 3, he pictures our deeds as materials built on Christ's foundation. Materials like gold, silver, and precious stones survive the test and bring reward; worthless materials like wood or straw burn up. Obedience produces reward; disobedience means a loss of reward, though the person himself is saved (1 Cor 3:13-15).

Categories of Eternal Rewards

Scripture does not leave us guessing about what these eternal wages will be. In my book on the topic, I identify six categories of eternal rewards—riches, rights, recognition, regalia, royalty, and relationship. Each category is linked to specific promises in Scripture:

Riches. Jesus urged His disciples to "lay up for yourselves treasures in heaven" rather than earthly wealth. He exhorted them to sell their possessions and give to the poor, promising a money bag "that does not grow old" and a treasure that cannot be stolen (Matt 6:19-20; Luke 12:33). Those who are faithful in small things will be entrusted with "true riches" (Luke 16:11).

Rights. Faithful believers will be granted privileges beyond the gifts all believers receive. Revelation promises that the faithful will eat from the tree of life, become pillars in God's temple with His name written on them and have special privileges in to the holy city (Rev 2:7; 3:12; 22:14). By contrast, rights such as citizenship in heaven (Phil 3:20), glorified bodies (Phil 3:21) and adoption as children of God (John 1:12) are free gifts for all believers.

Recognition. Jesus promised to give public recognition to those with high performance in the Christian life. He will commend them before the Father (Matt 10:32-33). In the parable of the minas, He commends the servant who was faithful, "Well done, good servant..." (Luke 19:17). Jesus also said, "...If anyone serves me, the Father will honor him. (John 12:26)

Regalia. The faithful will receive crowns and garments signifying victory. James wrote that those who love the Lord under trial will receive the "crown of life," and Paul looked forward to the "crown of righteousness" promised to all who love Christ's appearing (James 1:12; 2 Tim 4:8). Revelation urges believers to hold fast so that no one may take their crown (Rev 3:11). Overcomers are promised white garments and a new name written on them. Other passages describe the crown of rejoicing (1 Thess 2:19), the imperishable crown (1 Cor 9:25), and the crown of glory (1 Pet 5:4).

Royalty. Those who endure will share in Christ's royal reign. Peter calls believers "a royal priesthood" (1 Pet 2:9), and Jesus promises authority over the nations to those who keep His works to the end (Rev 2:26). John sees saints reigning with Christ for a thousand years (Rev 20:6), and Paul reminds believers that they will judge the world and even angels (1 Cor 6:23). Daniel foretold that the kingdom would be given to the saints of the Most High (Dan 7:18), and Revelation declares that Christ has made us kings and priests to our God (Rev 5:10).

Relationship. The deepest reward is intimate fellowship with Christ. God told Abram, "I am your shield, your exceedingly great reward" (Gen 15:1). Jesus said, "You are My friends if you do whatever I command you" (John 15:14). Revelation promises that overcomers will dine with the risen Lord and sit with Him on His throne (Rev 3:20-21), receive hidden manna and a white stone with a new name

(Rev 2:17), and be pillars in the temple of God with His name and the name of the New Jerusalem written on them (Rev 3:12). The morning star—Christ Himself—will be given to the faithful (Rev 22:16).

These categories highlight how Heaven's rewards are not a generic pat on the back; they are a multifaceted compensation package—resources to steward, privileges to exercise, honors to receive, authority to wield, and, above all, a deeper relationship with our Savior. Understanding these categories helps us see that obedience now leads to real advantages in the kingdom to come.

Motivation Matters

At one point in my life, I remember asking myself, "I know I'm saved, so why should I try to live like a saint?" The answer came when I learned about eternal rewards. Understanding that obedience today yields compensation forever provided the motivation I needed.

Everyone needs motivation. You work for a paycheck; you exercise to lose weight. God designed you to be motivated by incentives. He encoded us to expect a payout, a consequence, an equal and opposite reaction. Winners are motivated; champions have passion; victors have incentives. Give everyone a trophy for participation, and the talent will dry up. Offer a substantial reward, and everyone will want to play. Action and motivation are married.

If you've believed in Jesus and received the free gift of salvation, your eternal home is guaranteed. But your success as a disciple isn't. You will either be a Christian winner or a Christian loser. Being a loser doesn't jeopardize salvation, but it does bring consequences. What's the difference between winners and losers? Motivation. Those who understand what's at stake are far more likely to live victoriously.

Eternal Security and the Early Church

VALTTERI LAHTI

"Believers in once saved, always saved invariably take the high ground historically as though they're defending the historic faith. This is incredibly dishonest. That's because before Augustine's novel teachings in the early 5th century, absolutely no one in the early church believed in once saved, always saved. I know of no patristic scholar or church historian who disputes that fact." ~David Bercot

Introduction

The documentary makes several claims regarding the historicity of the doctrine of eternal security. Among these claims is the assertion that no early Christian taught this doctrine until Augustine (AD 354–430) came to formulate it in the early 5th century. Another claim posits that the doctrine was exclusively taught among the Gnostics—a collective term for various heretical groups that rejected the Old Testament writings and held the belief that the creator of the universe was an evil "demiurge," from whom Jesus (viewed as a distinct deity in Gnosticism) came to save humanity. They also often denied the incarnation by teaching Docetism, thus denying that Jesus physically died on the cross.

Hard to Draw Definite Conclusions

When examining the earliest Christian writings, it becomes challenging to draw definitive conclusions concerning their understanding of salvation. Many of their works are short, and clear interpretations are elusive, given that these letters were not intended as complex theological treatises but rather as sources of moral encouragement.

Take Polycarp, for instance. In Chapter 1 of his Letter to the Philippians, he emphasizes salvation through faith rather than works, yet later suggests the necessity of perseverance to reign with Christ. This leaves some room for interpretation regarding whether Polycarp viewed reigning as a distinct reward from salvation or not.

Similar uncertainties arise when analyzing other early Christian works like the First Epistle of Clement and the Epistle to Diognetus.

The Odes of Solomon

Nevertheless, the early Jewish Christian text, the "Odes of Solomon," may include one of the earliest extrabiblical references to eternal security. Dating back to approximately AD 70-125, these poetic hymns depict salvation as "incorruptible" (Ode 17:2), possibly suggesting belief in a steadfast and unchangeable state of grace. Additionally, passages such as "For that which You gave, You gave freely, so that no longer will You draw back and take them again" (Ode 4:13) may imply the irrevocability of salvation.

Despite the book's poetic nature, its thematic consistency regarding the freeness of salvation, as evident in multiple passages such as in Ode 25:12, Ode 5:3, and Ode 29:5-6, possibly supports the notion of eternal security.[1]

While some scholars previously have attributed the Odes of Solomon to the 3rd century with heretical origins, modern scholarship more often situates them within Jewish Christian circles, written by a convert from the Essene community to Christianity in the late 1st or early 2nd century. Therefore, the comments of the Odes should not be disregarded as heretical.

---

[1] *Odes of Solomon*, translated by James Charlesworth, accessed May 26, 2025, https://earlychristianwritings.com.

Augustine

Augustine of Hippo towers over Western thought. His teachings differed from the modern understandings of eternal security. He taught the idea that God gives the "gift of perseverance" to only certain individuals who had received God's grace, securing their eternal salvation but not that of every believer. According to Augustine, assurance of salvation is not attainable until one has persevered to the end. That contradicts the scriptural understanding of assurance.

While his doctrine could be labeled "eternal security for the elect," Augustine did not assert that every individual who has received God's grace is truly elect, having the gift of perseverance. As he articulates in his writings: "For we are speaking of that perseverance whereby one perseveres unto the end, and if this is given, one does persevere unto the end; but if one does not persevere unto the end, it is not given, which I have already sufficiently discussed above."[2] This perspective diverges from Free Grace theology, and therefore, I will not be defending the points of Augustine or their historical validity, although Augustine did suggest that earlier figures like Cyprian (AD 210 to 258) held similar beliefs.

Nevertheless, within early Christianity, there were proponents of views similar to Free Grace theology.

Early Proponents

A significant movement within the early church viewed justification as solely contingent upon individual faith in Jesus Christ, impervious to loss through sinful deeds. Although Augustine challenged their interpretations of the New Testament and even created a treatise to critique their beliefs, he did not consider them to be outside the body of Christ. Augustine employed the Latin term "catholic"—not yet used in reference to the Roman Catholic Church but used by writers of his time to denote the unified body of Christ—to describe them. Augustine's acknowledgment of their existence is clear in his works, such as in the *City of God*, Book 21:

---

[2] Philip Schaff, *St. Augustine: Anti-Pelagian Writings*, vol. 5 of *Nicene and Post-Nicene Fathers, Series 1* (Peabody, MA: Hendrickson, n.d.), 1410.

> But, say they, the catholic Christians have Christ for a foundation, and they have not fallen away from union with Him, no matter how depraved a life they have built on this foundation, as wood, hay, stubble; and accordingly the well-directed faith by which Christ is their foundation will suffice to deliver them some time from the continuance of that fire, though it be with loss, since those things they have built on it shall be burned.[3]

Furthermore, Augustine mentions in the same book that some individuals he knew of taught that even apostates who became heretical are promised salvation from damnation:

> "But let us now reply to those who promise deliverance from eternal fire, not to the devil and his angels (as neither do they of whom we have been speaking), nor even to all men whatever, but only to those who have been washed by the baptism of Christ, and have become partakers of His body and blood, no matter how they have lived, no matter what heresy or impiety they have fallen into."[4]

Belief in eternal security within the early church was also recognized to have existed by the church historian J.N.D. Kelly in his book *Early Christian Doctrines*, where he noted multiple understandings of the doctrine in the early church, including the writer Jerome of Stridon (AD 347–420) within the same group mentioned by Augustine. Kelly expounded on his soteriology, stating:

> Jerome develops the same distinction, stating that, while the Devil and the impious who have denied God will be tortured without remission, those who have trusted in Christ, even if they have sinned and

---

[3] Augustine, *City of God and Christian Doctrine*, vol. 2 of *Nicene and Post-Nicene Fathers, Series 1* (Peabody, MA: Hendrickson, n.d.), 1065.
[4] Augustine, *City of God and Christian Doctrine*, vol. 2 of *Nicene and Post-Nicene Fathers, Series 1* (Peabody, MA: Hendrickson, n.d.), 1062.

fallen away, will eventually be saved. Much the same teaching appears in Ambrose, developed in greater detail.[5]

While Jerome seems to have believed in the possibility of temporal punitive consequences even after death, he nonetheless appears to have taught the fundamental concept of eternal security. Jerome's inclusion in the group which Augustine critiqued seems to have even been acknowledged by the Catholic historian Gregory Lombardo:

> Augustine, however, does not mention any names, and there is no evidence either here or in any other place that he is referring to these passages from the works of Jerome. Nevertheless, both Jerome and Ambrose seemed to have shared in the not uncommon error of their time, namely, that all Christians would sooner or later be reunited to God, an error which Augustine refutes here and in a number of other places.[6]

Thus, belief in eternal security was not merely the doctrine of a few marginal figures but seems to have been embraced by significant early thinkers such as Jerome, who taught that a justified believer cannot lose their justification due to sinful deeds.

Some understanding of eternal security was also possibly taught by the early Christian Jovinian, who died due to old age in the year 405. Though the extant writings of Jovinian are fragmented, certain comments he made suggest him having an understanding of eternal security. Church historian Philip Schaff argued that Jovinian likely taught the Calvinistic doctrine of the perseverance of the saints. Schaff remarked, "Jovinian's second point bears an apparent affinity with the Augustinian and Calvinistic doctrine of the *perseverantia sanctorum*. However, he does not explicitly attribute it to the eternal and unchangeable counsel of God."[7]

---

[5] J. N. D. Kelly, *Early Christian Doctrines*, 2nd ed. (New York: Harper & Row, 1960), 484.

[6] Augustine, *On Faith and Works*, trans. Gregory J. Lombardo (New York: Paulist Press, 1988), 64–65.

[7] Philip Schaff, *History of the Christian Church*, vol. 3 (New York: Charles Scribner's Sons, 1889), 197.

Nevertheless, Jovinian's statements, such as "Those who are once born again with full faith by baptism cannot be overcome by the devil," do not necessarily imply that every justified individual will persevere to the end as the Calvinistic doctrine of the perseverance of the saints would include. Instead, they may simply affirm that a justified individual cannot be overcome to the extent of losing their standing before God, not related to one's perseverance in the faith or in good works. Jovinian's surviving writings are too fragmented to draw clear conclusions, but it is plausible that he held an early understanding of eternal security.

It should also be noted that many see Jovinian's reference to baptism as spiritual baptism that occurs when one is born again through faith in Jesus, rather than water baptism. As Schaff also writes on Jovinian: "and makes a distinction between the mere baptism of water and the baptism of the Spirit." However, baptismal regeneration is not the primary topic of this writing.

Later Hints

Many similar statements exist in church history.

Caesarius of Arles, writing in the 5th century, acknowledges the existence of individuals similar to those referenced by Augustine in his Sermon 186, persisting even in his era.

Bede, a prominent figure of the late 7th century in England, also seems acquainted with the ongoing teaching of this doctrine.

An interesting comment, as noted by Jody Dillow, is made by Pseudo-Chrysostom in the 5th century.[8] This statement, compiled by Thomas Aquinas (1224-1274), presents an argument in Pseudo-Chrysostom's commentary on Matthew, advocating for a distinction between "reigning with Christ," considered a reward for service, and simply "being in the kingdom," which is unmerited. He writes,

> For a man to be in the kingdom is not to reign with Christ, but only to be numbered among Christ's people; what He says then of him that breaks the commandments is, that he shall indeed be reckoned

---

[8] Joseph C. Dillow, *Final Destiny: The Future Reign of the Servant Kings*, 3rd rev. ed. (Fort Worth, TX: Grace Theology Press, 2014), 275–76.

among Christians, yet the least of them. But he who enters into the kingdom, becomes partaker of His kingdom with Christ. Therefore, he who does not enter into the kingdom of heaven, shall not indeed have a part of Christ's glory, yet shall he be in the kingdom of heaven.[9]

Did Only Heretics Believed in Eternal Security?

As a final point that I believe needs to be addressed, there is the claim made by the documentary that during the ante-Nicene era, only the Gnostic heretical sects taught eternal security. As proof for this claim, they cited Origen, who did indeed say that the Gnostics taught some form of eternal security. Although it can be easily argued that even heretical sects may contain bits of truth, church historians have also noted that Origen appears to have knowledge of non-Gnostic Christian writers who taught the security of the believer. This is even acknowledged by the Roman Catholic scholar Thomas Scheck, who writes:

> Origen again shows awareness of persons who do not seem to be heretics, but who do not understand the inextricable link between faith and good works. He refers to them as he expounds Rom 10.9, where it is evident that Origen rejects their theology, insisting that belief in Christ's resurrection and public confession of his lordship profits one nothing if his resurrection is not realized in the life of the believer.[10]

Although Origen was hostile to the idea of eternal security, which was likely influenced by his allegorical hermeneutics, his writings demonstrate that the concept of eternal security existed within Christian circles during the Ante-Nicene period.

---

[9] Thomas Aquinas and John Henry Newman, *Catena Aurea: Commentary on the Four Gospels Collected out of the Works of the Fathers*, vol. 1, St. Matthew (Oxford: John Henry Parker, 1841).

[10] Thomas P. Scheck, *Origen: Commentary on the Epistle to the Romans, Books 1–5* (Washington, DC: Catholic University of America Press, 2001), 35.

Conclusion

In conclusion, the documentary's assertion that eternal security was Augustine's invention is untenable upon closer examination of the historical data. Furthermore, while it is true that certain early Christians, such as Origen, voiced opposition to eternal security, the broader early church did not categorize it as a heretical belief but rather recognized it as a non-heretical interpretation of salvation. Even figures like Augustine, who contested the Free Grace understanding of eternal security, acknowledged them as a part of the body of Christ.

SECTION 2

Key Passages

1 Corinthians 9:24-27

Luke Morrison

"In 1 Corinthians 9:24–27, I think you have one of the clearest passages in all the entire Bible that you could forfeit your salvation, because nobody's gonna doubt the Apostle Paul was saved." ~Joe Schimmel

Introduction

Can a believer lose their salvation? Can believers become cut off from Christ because they have failed to continue faithfully? Is once saved always saved a scam by the church to get more people to come in so they can receive more money?

A more severe set of questions may be hard to discover. These questions strike at the heart of the saving message and our security as believers. If these questions are answered incorrectly, the questioner may very well walk away in fear of messing up in their Christian walk that they become strict legalists and live in misery. I firmly believe that once Christians have believed in Jesus Christ for the salvation He offers, they cannot be cut off from that salvation. This article seeks to demonstrate that a believer can fail in ministry and become "disqualified," but this does not hinder their eternal salvation.

To prove the thesis of this article, I will examine the verse many conditional security believers point to as proof that we can lose salvation. They point to this verse and say that no one is safe if the apostle Paul could become disqualified. Yet, the term *adokimos* (disqualified), even though used in other places in Paul's writings to show a possibility of corrupt faith or unbelief,[1] does not mean Paul is worried about losing salvation here.

The argument that Paul was worried about losing his salvation in 1 Cor 9:24-27 is that the word *adokimos* means "disqualified from heaven." The surrounding context simply does not support this claim. In Biblical studies, context is king. If the context disproves a belief, then the belief should submit to the context and not vice versa.

Look at the Context

Looking at the context of the chapter, we see that Paul begins by speaking about being free. Free to do what? Well, free to eat all meats, even meats sacrificed to idols (cf., 1 Cor 8:1-13). While Paul argues that eating meats sacrificed to idols is nothing because there is only one God (1 Cor 8:6), he says if this makes one stumble, he would never eat food again (1 Cor 8:10-13). As the chapter begins, Paul says he is free (1 Cor 9:1). He can eat, drink, and have a believing wife (vv 3-4). Furthermore, Paul argues that he is free to receive remuneration for his ministry to the Corinthians but chose not to so as not to place a hindrance before the gospel (vv 6-15).

It appears that the apostle Paul desired to ensure that the gospel reached everyone, even if he had to forgo certain rights for this to happen. In fact, in v 19, Paul clearly says he is free in all things; he made himself a servant to all. Paul sets the stage for this passage to be about ministry, not salvation per se. He argues that he has given up his freedoms for the sake of the gospel and the church.

As mentioned above, the context flows nicely into the discussion about an athlete running and disciplining their body for the prize so they do not become disqualified. When one reads the context, the ultimate conclusion is that Paul was concerned about the people seeing him as a swindler rather than a minister of the gospel of Christ.

---

[1] Many conditionalists and even some Calvinistic scholars hold that since Paul used the same term in Rom 1:28 about God giving them over to a debased (*adokimos*) mind because of their unbelief, and in 2 Timothy 3:8 where Jannes and Jambres were unfit (*adokimos*) for the faith that this term means one is lost or "disqualified from inheriting the kingdom of God." Per, Andrew David Naselli, "1 Corinthians," in *Romans–Galatians*, vol. X, *ESV Expository Commentary* ed. Iain M. Duguid, James M. Hamilton Jr., and Jay Sklar (Wheaton, IL: Crossway, 2020), 302.

However, the context of a passage is found in the preceding verses and those that follow.

The following context found in chap. 10 discusses the Israelites who were cut off in the wilderness wanderings and those killed by the serpents, plagues, and sin in the wilderness (cf., Num 21:4-9; 25:1-18). The problem with taking the loss of those lives in the wilderness as the ultimate proof that one can lose salvation is that Moses was not allowed to enter the Promised Land either (c.f., Num 20:1-13). To make the death outside the Promised Land of the Israelites who refused to enter because of the report from the twelve spies, the serpents, or anything else a loss of salvation is to say Moses is in hell, too. No Biblically literate person believes Moses is in hell. To say the context from chap. 10 means someone can lose their salvation is weak at best and false at worst.

Since this is the case, then what does it mean to be *disqualified*?

The Meaning of "Disqualified"

As mentioned above, Paul was concerned about putting a hindrance between the gospel and all who would hear (1 Cor 9:12). This is the disqualified that he was concerned about. He feared that if he allowed his freedoms and rights to become more important than the gospel in his work as an apostle, he would become disqualified, unapproved, worthless, or useless *in ministry*. Verse 18 of this chapter clearly expresses this point when Paul wrote that his reward is preaching the gospel freely and not abusing his authority (1 Cor 9:18). I agree with Michael G. Vanlaningham in the *Moody Bible Commentary* when he stated, "The disqualification here refers to forfeiting the chance to serve effectively in the great gospel mission."[2] Vanlaningham further stated that the disciplined life Paul said he practiced did not typify the average life of the Corinthians and that "self-indulgent Christians should not expect to be effective in ministry."[3]

This argument fits well with the terminology Paul used in 2 Timothy, where he wrote that an approved workman zealously learned the word so he could rightly utilize it in ministry (2 Tim 2:15). The

---

[2] Michael G. Vanlaningham, "1 Corinthians," *The Moody Bible Commentary*, ed Michael Rydelnik, and Michael G. Vanlaningham. (Chicago, IL: Moody Publishers, 2014), 1788.
[3] Ibid.

word used for approved is *dokimos*, which indicates that *adokimos* is the opposite of that. We all know this from the simple term "atheist," which means one who does not believe in God, while "theist" means one who does believe in God. The "a" before "theist" makes it the negative of a theist's beliefs. The same is true of the Greek words *dokimos* and *adokimos*. Simply put, Paul did not want to be an unapproved workman but an approved one who served well and was an effective gospel minister.

A simple illustration may help. I don't mind a nice whiskey drink now and then. I believe this is a freedom I have in my Christian walk. Now, say I am working with people who struggle with alcoholism, and I still enjoy that drink now and then. If these people found out I drank some, they may justify in their minds that it is okay to drink, even though they cannot control their impulses to drink. I have disqualified my ministry to those people because I did not discipline myself away from drinking and placed a stumbling block before them. I became an ineffective minister because I did not stop something in my life for the sake of another. This is what Paul wrote in this verse about his ministry.

Simply put, just as athletes could eat anything they desired because they were free to do so, they did not because the event was more important to them than their desire to eat sweets and other junk. Paul sees the gospel as more important than anything else in life. Therefore, he disciplined himself to not do certain things to be effective, qualified, or unqualified. In this passage, Paul worries about an effective ministry, not a loss of salvation.

Romans 11

TIM NICHOLS

"In Romans chapter 11, Paul makes very clear declarations that you can absolutely forfeit your salvation." ~Joe Schimmel

Introduction

Living downstream from the Great Awakenings, we are conditioned to read the Bible in terms of heaven, hell, and eternal destiny. Often, this flattens a Biblical discourse that *includes* eternal destiny but discusses much more.

In Romans, Paul illustrates the wrath and righteousness of God in ways that are evident today. Paul is eager to preach the gospel to those who already believe it (Rom 1:15) because it saves them (Rom 1:16). If they already believe, why do they still need saving? He describes the wrath that falls on unrighteousness—consequences that happen in this world. Their thinking becomes futile, their hearts dark; they're gripped by foolishness they can't see. Since they suppressed knowledge of God, He gives them to their lusts (Rom 1:24), with predictable results (Rom 1:28-32). Notice, the passage doesn't promise them hell; that's not Paul's subject here. He's talking about destruction in this life—a destruction from which the gospel delivers us.

Those who disapprove of such sin don't fare better. In condemning wickedness, they reveal the law written on their hearts, and judged by that law, we all fail. Here, Paul discusses eternity: God will give eternal life to those who patiently continue doing good and visit tribulation and wrath on everyone who does evil...which is all of us. What hope could we have? None, if righteousness came through law-keeping... but it doesn't. Paul points us to Abraham, who was justified by faith in God, and David, who was forgiven and restored to a state of blessedness after committing grievous sin. We are justified, found righteous, simply by faith.

Saved from Wrath

There's more: "Much more then, having been justified by His blood, we shall be saved from wrath through Him" (Rom 5:9). Justified by Jesus' death, we will now be saved by His life.

The first thing to notice here is that "justified" and "saved" are not the same thing. Saved is *much more* than being justified. How does that work?

Paul explains that our heritage in Adam could give us only death, but our heritage in Christ gives us life; therefore, we ought to consider ourselves dead to sin and alive to God. If you give yourself to a sin, you're enslaved, so it's important to get your mental furniture properly arranged. However, mental furniture by itself doesn't deliver us; sin dwells in us, and we end up doing things we hate. "O wretched man that I am!" Paul cries out. "Who will deliver me from this dead body?" (Rom 7:24)

The answer is not another mental furniture remodel; it's divine intervention: "If the Spirit of Him who raised Christ from the dead dwells in you, He...will also give life to your mortal bodies through His Spirit who dwells in you." (Rom 8:11). Your unresurrected body remains subject to the Fall, but the Spirit makes the life of the resurrection available to you (as Paul will explain in the remainder of chapter 8), and absolutely nothing can separate you from the love of God. The gospel not only *justifies* you for eternity, but it also *saves* you from the present destruction that sin works in our lives. That's quite a promise...if God can be trusted.

Working with a Remnant

But can He? God once promised Israel complete restoration—both the northern and southern kingdoms—throughout the Old Testament prophets. And yet, at the time Paul is writing, the northern kingdom is so thoroughly scattered among the Gentiles that nobody knows where they went. The southern kingdom, while restored to her territory under Cyrus and allowed to exist by the Romans, still lives spiritually and physically far short of the promised restoration. Arguably, things got worse when Jesus came, since the nation compounded her sins by crucifying the Messiah.

What are we to make of God's promises in a mess like that?

Paul begins by showing that God has worked with a faithful remnant before (Rom 9:1-29) and is within His rights to involve the Gentiles even as Israel rejects the gospel (Rom 9:30–10:13). Paul then indicts Israel for rejecting the gospel (Rom 10:14-21), which raises the question of chapter 11: "Has God cast away His people?"

Cast Away?

"No!" Paul says. "I'm one of them!" As in Elijah's day, God has preserved a remnant by grace...but that's not all. Israel's stumbling sent the gospel to the Gentiles, who will in turn provoke the Jews to jealousy. Paul says, if Israel's fall is good news for the Gentiles, how much more their restoration! Meanwhile, Paul ministers to the Gentiles, which will eventually bring in the Jews.

Therein lies a temptation for the Gentiles (and the Roman church in particular). "The Jews screwed it up," we might say to ourselves, "and now we've taken over as the center of God's plan." Paul warns us specifically against this temptation to pride and complacency using the image of an olive tree. As grafted-in branches, we depend on the root into which we were grafted. We don't support the tree; the tree supports us. We aren't the center of anything. If the native branches were broken off because they were unfruitful, we have that much less reason to become complacent.

> **Therefore consider the goodness and severity of God: on those who fell, severity; but toward you, goodness, if you continue in His goodness. Otherwise you also will be cut off (Rom 11:22).**

Occasionally, you'll run into someone who takes Rom 11:22 out of context to say that an individual, once heaven-bound, will go to hell if they rebel against God. I hope you can see that this passage not only doesn't say that, but it adds up to the opposite! It isn't talking about individuals or heaven and hell, but rather our place in God's plan as part of a people group.

Paul invites us to a devotional contemplation of the theology he has explained. Our place in the scheme, as Gentiles, is to walk with God. As we continue to do that, we continue to participate in His plan. Israel has forfeited that opportunity, and so could we. (Individual Israelites can still come to Christ, as Paul has, and individual Gentiles could too, even if we were cut off as a group.) But even this forfeiture is temporary: they will be grafted back into their own tree in due time, "and so all Israel will be saved" (Rom 11:26), even the lost tribes who assimilated with the Gentiles, because God is also bringing the Gentiles back. The severity is a temporary measure, designed to restore Israel to her rightful salvation.

Again, remember what "saved" means here: "much more" than justification! It's deliverance from the consequences of sin in this life, too. It is precisely the kind of thing God promised Israel through the prophets, centuries before Christ: a heart of flesh rather than a heart of stone (Ezek 11:19), sons and daughters prophesying (Joel 2:28), every man knowing the Lord (Jer 31:34).

Conclusion

God is faithful to His promises. He will restore Israel. He will save those who trust in Him. He will discipline those who turn away to bring them back. Based on those rock-solid promises, we should be enthusiastic about Paul's next challenge to us: "I beseech you therefore, brethren, by the mercies of God, that you present your bodies a living sacrifice…" (Rom 12:1).

Hebrews 6:4–9

Daniel Goepfrich

"Hebrews has at least a dozen passages that refute once saved, always saved. Chapters 6 and 10 seem to just say bluntly, you can lose your salvation."
~Douglas Jacoby

Introduction

Of the five warning passages in the book of Hebrews, the third is the best known. It may be the second-best-known section of Hebrews, second only to the list of names in chapter eleven. This passage is also widely debated and requires careful attention for correct interpretation. While the warning is in Heb 6:4-8, the last paragraph of chapter five (Heb 5:11-14) and the first three verses of chapter six set the tone for the entire section, proving that the theme is about spiritual maturity, not eternal salvation.

The Need to Grow Beyond the Basics

The writer began with the understanding that his readers had made progress in their spiritual lives at one time, but they had become dull of hearing. They had stopped listening to and practicing the truth. Because of this, they digressed to the point of needing milk again rather than solid spiritual food. Although they had been believers long enough that some or all of them should have been able to be teachers by this time, they needed someone to teach them the basic principles again and press onward in their Christian growth.

"For it is impossible" presents the warning as the writer explained why deliberate spiritual maturity and growth should not be considered optional and why the readers needed to move beyond their elementary teachings.

"Enlightened…tasted…made partakers…tasted…and then have fallen away"– many have tried to make the case that these words describe someone close to salvation but not a true believer. However, when taken together, and primarily when understood in the broader context of Hebrews, we find a different story altogether. Here is how the writer used these exact words elsewhere in his letter:

- There was a specific point in these believers' past when they were enlightened, marking the distinction between their unbelief and belief in Jesus as Messiah (Heb 10:32).
- Jesus did "taste death for everyone" (Heb 2:9). He did not only sample death. He went through it entirely, came out the other side, and was changed because of it.
- These very same readers were "partakers of a heavenly calling" (Heb 3:1) and had "become partakers of Christ" (Heb 3:14) through their eternal salvation.

It is incomprehensible that the writer would use identical language for two completely different groups of people. The people described in this passage are unquestionably believers.

In chapter two, the writer warned his Christian readers about drifting away from the truth through negligence. Secondly, he warned them about having an unbelieving heart and failing to trust God. He now referred to the same apostasy in a third way.

The word translated "have fallen away" is *parapiptō* (to fall by the wayside), not the same word found in Heb 3:12. This word does not occur anywhere else in the New Testament, indicating that it is not an experience or state that is normal for a believer; it is an aberration, an anomaly, yet still a possibility.

For someone who truly falls away from his faith, "it is impossible…to restore [him] again to repentance." This signifies that the writer was no longer talking about just drifting. Falling away is the hardening of the unbelieving heart from the second warning. According to the writer, a believer can backslide or walk so far from God that he or she reaches a point of unbelief from which they can no longer repent and return to their previous state of maturity. In the case of the original audience of Hebrews, the point of no return was probably finalized with their physical deaths during the destruction of Jerusalem and the Temple in AD 70, just a few years later.

There Is a Point of No Return

This is a difficult teaching for many people to accept, and it would be easy to dismiss or reinterpret it if this were the only place we found this concept, but it is not. Jesus, James, Paul, and John also spoke about a point of no return for believers who leave the faith (cf. John 15:1-6; Jas 5:19-20; 1 Cor 11:27-32; 1 John 5:16-17). Each of these passages finds a believer who fails at some point in his spiritual maturity. Though the call is made to repent, in each case, they refuse to heed the call and find a point of no return, resulting in physical death.

It is important to reiterate that this is not about the renewal of forgiveness or eternal salvation. Eternal salvation was already secured when they believed in Jesus and does not need to be repeated. The entire context of Hebrews 5 and 6 is about the maturity of believers, not the salvation of unbelievers. The description is of a believer who veers off the path toward spiritual maturity, regressing to the status of an infant in need of milk but refusing even that. It is this individual—who knows better, who has experienced the goodness available through a growing relationship with Christ—who consciously chooses to discard it for his own physical safety and his own plan. This person is "not fit" to be associated with Jesus (Luke 9:57-62). He is to be removed from fellowship with the church (Matt 18:15-17) and turned back out into Satan's world where he thinks he wants to be (1 Cor 5:1-5; 1 Tim 1:18-20). The consequences of this choice are severe and should serve as a cautionary tale for all believers.

Is God Too Harsh?

Many have pushed hard against the point of no return. They argue, "Where is the grace, the love, the forgiveness? Is God so harsh that he would not allow them back? What if they didn't know what they were doing?" Knowing how hard this truth was for his readers (then and now!) to accept, the writer explained it differently.

He was clear that falling away from the faith is not a momentary lapse of judgment. It is not, "I made a mistake, but God won't let me return." This believer has not only "tasted the good word of God and the powers of the age to come" (v 5), but he also has had the rain of God's Word, blessing, and power frequently falling on him. This disciple was once on the path to maturity but began to wander. He spiraled further and further—drifting, neglecting, hardening his heart, rejecting the Father's loving discipline (12:5-13)—until he passed the point of a spiritual infant (where some of the immediate readers had already fallen, 5:11-14). Falling away is a road marked by spiritual apathy, resulting in the rejection of the Savior. Paul wrote that this type of person "has deviated from what is right and is sinning, being self-condemned" (Titus 3:11). This is not a one-time decision or instantaneous development that the person will regret the following day. It is a conscious, willful walking away from what he knows to be true.

On the other hand, growing, maturing believers will take God's blessings and turn them into "a crop useful"—great acts of worship and fruitful service for their Lord. Thorns and thistles come from a believer's heart not devoted to God. It was the cause of God's ancient lament, "These people say they are mine. They honor me with their lips, but their hearts are far from me" (Isa 29:13 NLT). It is the message of many of Jesus' teachings, the New Testament apostles' exhortations, and the Old Testament prophets' warnings.

Whereas the person who receives God's blessings and discipline provides useful vegetation, the one who continues rejecting Christ becomes useless. In 1 Cor 9:27, Paul used the same word (*adokimos*) to say that if he did not continue serving faithfully, he would disqualify himself. Nothing could make us believe that Paul feared for his eternal salvation. Instead, he did not want to lose the privilege of preaching the gospel he loved. He did not want to be disqualified or rejected from service in this life.

Near to Being Cursed

Contrary to how many people interpret this passage, the result of this falling away is not that the person is cursed. We might understand this as a loss of eternal salvation. The writer specifically claimed that the person would be near to being cursed. We could say he is as far from God and as close to being cursed as a true believer could ever be.

Again, the concept of burning leads people to think this means that the believer will go to hell, but neither the context nor the rest of the New Testament teaches this. The analogy is about the treatment of a piece of land, not a person. When a piece of land grows only thorns and weeds, no matter how the owner tries to rejuvenate it, sometimes the only solution is to burn it. This often results in the land being unable to grow anything again, but it does not change the fact that it is still earth. In the same way, the eternal state of the person remains unchanged; he or she is eternally saved. However, much like a burnt parcel of ground, the person will never again have the opportunity to produce anything useful for its owner. As shown by the Corinthian believers' abuse of the Lord's table and other passages above, this form of divine discipline may be premature physical death. The idea is further developed and applied to all believers in 1 Cor 3:10-15, where God will judge our works with his holy fire. The worthless results will be burnt up, while the person himself will be saved, even if he has nothing to show for his life and no inheritance in the kingdom.

Conclusion

In contrast to the common understanding that this passage teaches the loss of eternal salvation due to an unknown or arbitrary definition of falling away, we find a God who pursues his people, encouraging a growing relationship with him. However, if someone knowingly, willingly runs away, there is a point at which nothing in heaven or on earth could cause him to be restored to the fellowship he once enjoyed with God. The result is a life of misery, possibly a premature physical death, and a loss of reward in eternity. Yet even with all that, God will not curse him forever because there is "no condemnation at all for those who are in Christ Jesus" (Rom 8:1) because they have been "sealed for the day of redemption" (Eph 4:30). The Savior's eternal promise is that even "if we are faithless, He remains faithful, for He cannot deny Himself" (2 Tim 2:13). Our eternal salvation is given and kept by His faithfulness, not ours.

The application for the ancient readers is the same for us today: there is no such thing as a Christian on hold. We are either growing in our relationship with God or falling away from him. If we leave our relationship unchecked, maturity can become immaturity, apathy, and even outright rejection.

Hebrews 10:26-31

Jeremy Mikkelsen

"It's an a fortiori argument. If the Old Testament people of God could lose their salvation, given the greater privilege we have in the gospel, how much more severely would God deal with us?"
~Douglas Jacoby

Introduction

To those who believe that a person can lose their salvation, Hebrews 10:26-31 is likely one of the first passages they would point to make a Biblical argument against OSAS (once saved always saved):

> For if we deliberately go on sinning after we have received the knowledge of the truth, a sacrifice for sins no longer exists. Instead, there is only a certain fearful expectation of judgment, and a fury of fire that will consume God's enemies. Anyone who has rejected the law of Moses dies without mercy at the testimony of two or three witnesses. How much worse punishment do you think one deserves who has trampled underfoot the Son of God, who treated the blood of the covenant as unholy—the blood by which he was sanctified—and insulted the Spirit of grace? For we know the one who said, "Vengeance belongs to me; I will pay back." And again, "The Lord will judge his people." It is a fearful thing to fall into the hands of the living God! (Heb 10:26-31 ULB)

Out of context, without understanding the history, it is easy to understand it to be saying that you can lose your salvation. But if this passage is not talking about losing your salvation, I would suggest to you that rest of the anti-OSAS passages are even less convincing.

The Author Includes Himself

Let's start with the obvious, and something that non-OSAS believers would agree with. The author is including himself in the audience of the warning: **If *we* deliberately go on sinning...** It is not addressed to "you all" but to "we." It should be apparent from the very beginning of the book that it is addressed to believers, particularly Hebrew (i.e., Jewish) people in the first century. Any claim by those who teach POTS (perseverance of the saints) that this warning applies only to "non-believers" is neither faithful to the text nor logical. It is nonsensical to warn a "non-believer" about any sanctification issue. We should rather be warning them about the white throne judgment, i.e., the lake of fire.

We All Deliberately Sin

The second issue should be obvious, if we are honest. *We all still deliberately sin.* I do. And so do you. The apostle John tells us as much in 1 John 1:8: "If we say that we have no sin, we are deceiving ourselves, and the truth is not in us." Unless you think that everyone— believers and unbelievers alike—should expect **"a certain fearful expectation of judgement, and a fury of fire,"** I suspect most would agree there is a particular tier or type of sin that this refers to. Lots of legalistic churches have a list of which sins are "bad" enough to cancel your salvation. But have you ever asked yourself, what was the specific sin that the author of the book of Hebrews had in mind when he (or she) wrote this? Rather than just make up new rules (like the Pharisees did), perhaps we should examine the context to see if we can figure out the original concern.

The Original Concern

The first half of the book of Hebrews is focused on "Jesus is Better"—better than the prophets, better than the angels, better than

Moses, better than Aaron.

The second section is focused on how the New Covenant is better—better promises, better sanctuary, and a better sacrifice.

Then, finally, the third section contains exhortations and applications. Hebrews 10:26-31 occurs toward the beginning of this third section.

Looking at the immediate context, you might notice a pattern. What is the author describing?

> Those who approach God can never be made perfect by the same sacrifices that the priests continually bring year after year (Heb 10:1).
>
> ...or it is impossible for the blood of bulls and goats to take away sins (Heb 10:4).
>
> ...He takes away the first practice in order to establish the second practice. By that will, we have been sanctified through the offering of the body of Jesus Christ once for all. Day after day every priest stands and performs his service to God. He offers the same sacrifices again and again—sacrifices that can never take away sins (Heb 10:9-11).
>
> Now where there is forgiveness for these, there is no longer any sacrifice for sin (Heb 10:18).
>
> That is the new and living way that he has opened for us through the curtain, that is, by means of his flesh (Heb 10:20).

You should go read the whole chapter to be sure, but the author is talking about how Hebrew believers in the Messiah were to stop performing the old temple sacrifices.

Think about it. If you were a "Christian" Jew before AD 70, you had a hard choice in front of you: trust in Jesus and face certain persecution, or keep quiet and continue to make the old temple sacrifices and avoid persecution. The main point of the exhortation is pretty clear:

> Let us also hold tightly to the confession of our hope without wavering, because God, who has promised, is faithful (Heb 10:23).

The confession is that Jesus' one sacrifice for sin was sufficient. So, what happens if a believer, the "Christian" Hebrew, stops meeting together (v 25), and resumes the temple worship and sacrifices? This confession goes out the window. That is what this warning is all about!

> For if we deliberately go on sinning after we have received the knowledge of the truth, a sacrifice for sins no longer exists (Heb 10:26).

Once you believe in Jesus, doing the temple sacrifices for sin does not do anything for you and your sin. Rather, it becomes a sin of denying Christ.

> "Instead, there is only a certain fearful expectation of judgment, and a fury of fire that will consume God's enemies" (Heb 10:27).

The Hebrew believer who has gone back to temple worship should expect judgment because they are actively denying Christ in the process.

> Anyone who has rejected the law of Moses dies without mercy at the testimony of two or three witnesses. How much worse punishment do you think one deserves who has trampled underfoot the Son of God, who treated the blood of the covenant as unholy—the blood by which he was sanctified—and insulted the Spirit of grace? (Heb 10:28-29)

If those who rejected the law of Moses die without mercy on the testimony of a couple of witnesses, what would you expect to happen if you reject the Christ by performing meaningless temple "sacrifices"? By offering these sacrifices (motivated by a desire to avoid persecution), they were denying Christ. A witness won't be required, because

God himself will judge you with death. Indeed, if you study the history of what happened in 70 AD, all those who remained connected to the temple met a particularly gruesome (and fiery) death. Whereas those who fled Jerusalem due to persecution mostly survived.

Identifying the Stakes

Now lots of people want to make this consequence to be hell rather than just "death." However, hell is absent from the context entirely. The issue at hand is not justification—this is not dealing with the free gift of salvation by grace through faith (cf. Eph 2:8-9). The issue at hand is how they are going to survive the trial of persecution. What follows the warning is contextually vital to understand.

> **But remember the former days, after you were enlightened, how you endured a great struggle in suffering. You were exposed to public ridicule by insults and persecution, and you were sharing with those who went through such suffering. For you had compassion on those who were prisoners, and you accepted with joy the seizure of your possessions. You knew that you yourselves had a better and everlasting possession. So do not throw away your confidence, which has a great reward (Heb 10:32-35).**

Identifying what is at stake is so critical. Here are the options the author of Hebrews offers the original audience:

Option 1: Keep doing temple sacrifices, avoid earthly persecution now, but in the future face the wrath of God—death (when Roman general Titus shows up) and loss of reward in Christ's kingdom when He returns.

Option 2: Endure earthly persecution as a witness for Christ, with faith and hope of a great reward in Christ's kingdom when He returns.

This paradigm is not unique to Hebrews. These same options parallel the middle part of Paul's "trustworthy saying" in 2 Tim 2:12, i.e.,

If we endure, we reign with Him; If we deny Him, we will be denied (i.e., denied the reward of reigning).

The author of Hebrews then offers a paraphrase of Habakkuk 2, especially vv 3-4 as evidence that Jesus will return, and that the faithful will honored and that those who do not will not be.

> **For in a very little while, the one who is coming will indeed come and not delay. My righteous one will live by faith. If he shrinks back, I will not be pleased with him (Heb 10:38; cf. Hab 2:3-4).**

Saving What?

A final conclusion to this thought is then recorded in the final verse of chapter 10. However, it is often poorly translated. Here is the traditional rendering:

> **But we are not any of those who turn back to destruction. Instead, we are some of those who have faith *for keeping our soul* (Heb 10:39, emphasis added).**

The basic gist is pretty simple: those who go back to the temple worship are actually going back to destruction. Perhaps this language is figurative. However, I would suggest it is specifically referring to what the Roman general Titus did to Jerusalem and its inhabitants. Instead, the author and hopefully his believing audience will "save their life." Now, if you are not a regular student of Greek, you might be wondering why I wrote "save their *life*" rather than "save their *soul*." It is because the Greek word used here, *psyche*, can mean either. Here is what a prominent lexicon (BDAG) states the definition as:

> psyche (ψυχή) ('life, soul') It is often impossible to draw hard and fast lines in the use of this multivalent word...
> ① life on earth in its animating aspect making bodily function possible
>   ⓐ *(breath of) life, life-principle, soul,* of animals

  ⓑ the condition of being alive, *earthly life, life* itself
  ⓒ by metonymy, *that which possesses life/soul*
 ② seat and center of the inner human life in its many and varied aspects, *soul*
  ⓐ of the desire for luxurious living
  ⓑ of evil desires
  ⓒ of feelings and emotions
  ⓓ as the seat and center of life that transcends the earthly
  ⓔ Since the soul is the center of both the earthly (1a) and the transcendent (2d) life, pers. can find themselves facing the question concerning the wish to ensure it for themselves
 ③ an entity w. personhood, *person* extension of 2 by metonymy

  This is why various translations render this final verse rather differently. For example, the Holman Christian Standard Bible renders it this way: "But we are not those who draw back and are destroyed, but those who have faith *and obtain life*" (emphasis added). Still other translations purposely leave it vaguer, e.g., NIV: "But we do not belong to those who shrink back and are destroyed, but to those who have faith *and are saved*" (emphasis added).

  So yes, this passage is all about saving your "soul," but the author is not talking about anyone's eternal salvation. Rather the author is trying to save the physical lives (and the testimony) of some people who are fearing people rather than God.

Applying This Passage Today

  We will wrap up by examining the applications to a modern audience. We do not face the particular situation of being pressured to participate in Jewish temple worship or face persecution. However, the underlying principle—are we going to fear man or God?—is very relevant today. In most Muslim places around the world, believers have to choose between persecution or living their faith privately. Hebrews teaches us to fear God rather than people.

  As our freedoms here in the West continue to erode, we too may face a day where we have to decide between obeying and following

God or keeping our lives "easy." Increasing persecution will pressure many to give up on a public display of their faith. We observed during COVID just how relevant Heb 10:25 is in light of governmental intrusion (e.g., "Let us not stop meeting together, as some have done"). Failure to heed this warning could be very dangerous for many believers.

But when teachers turn this passage into a warning about losing one's salvation, at best, their audience will miss its intended purpose of keeping believers strong in the face of persecution. At worst, they can get stuck in a form of legalism that teaches your eternal salvation is based on your church attendance and not "sinning" the really "bad sins." That is a very different gospel indeed.

2 Peter 2:20-22

Eli Haitov

"Peter says it would have been better for them never to have known the way of righteousness than to have known it and turned away. That is talking about someone forfeiting their salvation."
~Michael Brown

Introduction

Does this passage teach conditional security? Some think it does. However, a close reading of the text, in its wider and immediate context, negates this view.

Two Different Groups

To understand the passage properly, we must first understand the identity of those who "have escaped the pollutions of the world through the knowledge of the Lord and Saviour Jesus Christ."

The chapter begins with discussing the fate of the unsaved false teachers (vv 1-17). Then, in v 18, Peter tells us that those false teachers "allure through the lusts of the flesh, through much wantonness, those that were clean escaped from them who live in error." Thus, those who have escaped the pollutions of the world, are not identical with the unsaved false teachers that are discussed in the previous context. Rather, this is a separate group of people who deviate from a life of holiness.

Textual clues suggest that this group represents saved people. In the first chapter, Peter writes to his saved audience that "his divine power hath given unto us all things that pertain unto life and godliness, through the knowledge of him that hath called us to glory and virtue...having escaped the corruption that is in the world through lust" (vv 3-4). You can see the shared language here. This shared language refers to saved people who have escaped positionally from the power of sin (who are potentially now are being enslaved to it again experientially). These are believers.

Moreover, Peter tells us in chapter 2 that this group of people (who are being allured by the false teachers) has escaped the pollutions of the world through the knowledge of the Lord and Savior Jesus Christ (v 20). The word "knowledge" here is the same word that appears in chap. 1, v 2: "Grace and peace be multiplied unto you through the knowledge of God, and of Jesus our Lord." The word is *epignōsei* and according to Thayer's lexicon, one of its primary meanings is "to become thoroughly acquainted with, to know thoroughly; to know accurately, know well."[1] That is, in Peter's view, these are mature believers. Not fake ones, nor are they even immature believers.

The Fate of These Believers

The real issue, however, is their fate. Does Peter talk about Hell? Does he say it would have been better for them to have never been saved? No. Their latter state does not refer to eternal condemnation.

Peter talks about their *initial* moral state versus their *last* moral state. More specifically, he refers to their initial moral state as babes in Christ, that is, before their experience with sanctification, versus their latter state as saved people after falling to a polluted lifestyle. The fact that Peter does not discuss eternal condemnation here is clear from his allusion to Prov 26:11: "As a dog returneth to his vomit, so a fool returneth to his folly." The passage in Proverbs does not discuss eternal Hell. Rather, it discusses moral character. The point is that those who have progressed in the path of righteousness would be better off not doing it if they return to a sinful lifestyle. Their latter moral state is worse than their initial moral state as new believers.[2]

---

[1] https://biblehub.com/greek/1921.htm

[2] Hodges, "2 Peter," 582.

Thus, Peter does not say that it would have been better for these kinds of believers to have never been saved. Rather, he says that it would have been better for them not to have been experientially sanctified if they went back to their former lifestyle. Because now their moral character is even worse. "To have known the way of righteousness" does not refer to positional righteousness received through faith in Christ. Rather, the way of righteousness is defined in this context as the way of moral righteousness.[3] Or as someone puts it, it is the kingdom way of living.

Conclusion

This passage does not warn us from losing our salvation. Rather, it warns us from becoming worse than we have begun, morally speaking. As Dillow puts it, "The passage is a severe warning to those being enticed to return to their former ways of sin, but there is nothing here about loss of salvation."[4]

---

[3] Schreiner, "1, 2 Peter, Jude," 362

[4] Dillow, *Final Destiny: The Future Reign of The Servant Kings* Revised Edition, 670.

James 5:19-20

Shawn Willson

"James is yet another incredibly clear passage about forfeiture of salvation—a strong warning."
~Joe Schimmel

Introduction

Living in New Orleans, Louisiana, I have seen the force of hurricane winds firsthand. In 2021, Hurricane Ida moved over southeast Louisiana with category four sustained winds of nearly 150 mph, passing right over my home and church. Thankfully, the Lord protected the people and possessions of my local church, but the devastation across the community was shocking and awe-inspiring.

Trees were ripped up from their roots and homes torn in half. Cars were flipped onto their sides. Telephone poles snapped like popsicle sticks. It is one thing to watch a news report of storm damage, and it is something else entirely to walk through your own neighborhood after such an incredible force has struck.

As devastating as a hurricane can be, sin wrecks more lives, families, and communities than any other force on earth. Natural disasters are nothing before the destructive power of the unnatural works of sin that have invaded God's good creation and wreaked havoc on the lives of both believers and unbelievers alike. For this reason, the Bible consistently uses the strongest of terms to call on God's people to avoid sin in every form.

Many of those warning passages have led people in the church to believe that sinful practices not only ruin the physical lives of God's people but will strip believers of their eternal life provided by Christ and the sealing of the Spirit upon their lives. One of those warning passages is Jas 5:19-20. In this passage, James works to impress upon his readers the importance of not only avoiding sin for one's own benefit but also helping a fellow Christian avoid sinful ruin.

If Any Among You Strays

My brethren, if any among you strays from the truth and one turns him back, let him know that he who turns a sinner from the error of his way will save his soul from death and will cover a multitude of sins (Jas 5:19-20).

While James writes to protect the sinning Christian from the consequences of iniquity that fall upon the guilty, this passage also touches on the debate between eternal and conditional security. Each side of the debate asks the Bible student to discern what form of death James refers to in v 20 when he writes on saving "his soul from death"? Does James refer to eternal separation from God and the loss of eternal life for the brethren of v 19 or does James warn of physical death as a consequence of sin? What is the most likely understanding of death in James's admonition? Is this physical or spiritual death?

James only uses death in one other verse in his letter which is v 15: "Then, when desire has conceived, it gives birth to sin; and sin, when it is full-grown, brings forth death." The warning in Jas 1:15 is similar to the instruction in Jas 5:19-20. The similarities are found both in the warning of possible death and the lack of details tied to the warning of possible death. The interpreter can only be certain of one truth with regards to James' writing on sin and death. Sin brings death.

Sadly, for many students of Scripture, a superficial examination of Jas 1:15 and 5:19-20 ends the discussion. Sin obviously brings eternal death or separation from God forever, so there is no need even to consider the physical death option. This rash decision would be a mistake, because James does not explicitly refer to eternal condemnation in either passage. Rushing to a judgment of eternal condemnation would place words into James' instruction that are not present in the Biblical text. When the Word of God as a whole is examined, death refers to both physical death and eternal separation from God. There are two forms of death. One is physical and one is spiritual.

The Results of Sin

Beginning with Adam and Eve in the garden, sin resulted not only in separation from God but also physical death. The easy majority of uses for the Greek word *thanatos,* used for death in James, refer to physical and not spiritual death throughout the New Testament. James writes on death coming on account of sin. This does not limit the interpreter to view the death as eternal condemnation since death has two uses in the New Testament. James's use of sin bringing death also does not limit the interpreter to spiritual death, as sin brings physical death on several occasions.

A clear example of physical death as the result of sin comes from Matt 15:4, "For God commanded, saying, 'Honor your father and your mother'; and, 'He who curses father or mother, let him be put to death.' The death resulting from cursing one's father or mother according to the Mosaic Law is capital punishment or physical death. James is from a Jewish worldview where it was typical to view physical death as a result of sin.

James also writes that the one who turns the sinner "will save his soul from death." Does saving one's soul from death point toward saving one's spiritual life from condemnation at the Great White Throne Judgment, or can the salvation of the soul also refer to physical life? Soul or *psuche* is used approximately 100 times in the New Testament. There are ample occasions where the soul refers to an individual's physical life on this earth.

In Matt 2:20, the angel tells Joseph to return to Israel, because those who sought the soul of Jesus are dead. In Matt 6:20, Jesus tells us that our soul is more than what we eat, referring to our lives in this world. In Acts 27:22, Paul prophecies that no souls will be lost on the ship carrying him to Rome. This is clearly referring to the salvation of the lives of both passengers and sailors during the upcoming shipwreck. In Rom 11:3, Paul quotes the words of Elijah from 1 Kgs 19:10 where Elijah complains that Jezebel is seeking his soul. She desires to kill him. Paul also writes about Epaphroditus in Phil 2:25-30. He informs the church of Philippi that Epaphroditus risked his soul in service to Christ.

There is a reason that exact quotes were not provided for the passages in the paragraph above. Modern English translations consistently translated *psuche* as *life* instead of *soul*. Our English translations have influenced the modern Christian's understanding of the soul as used in the New Testament. The soul clearly refers to one's physical in many passages. If the English translations were consistent in their translation of *psuche*, the student of the Word would more easily see that *psuche* should be first be understood as physical life and only secondarily be seen as one's eternal spiritual life if the context demands it. When a soul is saved in the New Testament, it is the physical life of the individual who is saved, as seen in the Christ child, Paul, Elijah, and Epaphroditus.

Conclusion

In spite of the many uses of psuche for the loss of physical life, the interpreter cannot be completely confident in an interpretation of the loss of physical life. This is due to the use of death of the soul for both physical and spiritual death (see Matt 10:28 for a use of spiritual death). Sin also causes both physical and spiritual death. The overall usage of psuche combined with killing or death points to the loss of physical, but this is not the exclusive meaning of the death of the soul. For this reason, James should be understood as providing a simple admonition in Jas 5:19-20. Those who keep their siblings in Christ from a sinful lifestyle protect them from sin and all of its consequences, including death.

Jas 5:19-20 should be kept out of the debate regarding whether a Christian can forsake or lose their salvation. James is not speaking to that issue. Instead, he is calling on Christians to help one another turn from sinful practices so we may save them from all the consequences of sin that may fall upon a believer in Christ.

I do not believe one consequence of sin is eternal separation from God in hell. John 3:16 alone promises every believer protection from perishing on account of sin, thanks to the eternal life of Christ in us. This protection from Christ's life in us does not guarantee that our physical lives will not be destroyed and ruined to the point of death in this life by sin. Therefore, I see Jas 5:19-20 as a call for Christians to protect one another from physical loss on account of sin.

Those who hold to a view that a believer can forsake their salvation in sin and return to the threat of condemnation and the judgment of perishing will obviously see both forms of death (physical and spiritual) present in Jas 5:19-20. The point of this exposition on Jas 5:19-20 is not to argue for eternal security or conditional security, but to demonstrate that James does not provide ammunition for either side of the debate.

Both sides of this debate should agree that James calls on every Christian to protect their brothers and sisters in Christ from the dangers of sin, because sin is a destructive, life-killing force in the lives of all people, believers and unbelievers alike.

So What Is "Salvation" in James?

Chris Morrison

"That that word *psychē* is used one other time in the book of James in relationship to the truth and salvation. And that's where James says to receive the word engrafted, which is able to save your souls, your *psychē*. So we're talking about spiritual salvation here, which can be lost as James points out." ~Joe Schimmel

Introduction

James asks, "What good is it, my brothers, if a man says he has faith, but has no works? Can faith *save* him?" (Jas 2:14 WEB). What we think "salvation" refers to here will fundamentally determine how we interpret the passage.

Lexical Evidence

Before we answer the question, we should just stop and ask what the *word* "save" (Greek, *sōzō*) means. The BDAG—the standard Greek lexicon—gives two basic meanings: "To preserve or rescue from natural dangers and afflictions, save, keep from harm, preserve, rescue"; and "to save or preserve from transcendent danger or destruction, save/preserve from eternal death." Notice that these correspond to temporal and eternal salvation. It also maps onto common sense. If I ask a lifeguard to save me from drowning, I'm not asking him to take me to heaven to see Jesus. Just the opposite!

Sōzō in James

Of course, just because *sōzō can* mean either save from hell or save from some temporal danger, it doesn't follow that it has to mean either in any given passage. And it's always a bad idea to let our theology or tradition decide which usage is intended in Jas 2:14 (or any other verse). One way to decide the question is to examine how the word is used in its immediate context.

Unfortunately, I'm going to admit that the immediate context is ambiguous. There are good reasons to think that salvation is temporal, but this passage has been so widely interpreted as referring to eternal salvation that I can't, in good faith, say that the context alone settles the question. But before we give up, we can ask if and how James uses *sōzō* in the rest of the book. In fact, we see he uses the term four other times:

> Therefore, putting away all filthiness and overflowing of wickedness, receive with humility the implanted word, which is able to save [*sōzō*] your souls (Jas 1:21).

> Only one is the lawgiver, who is able to save [*sōzō*] and to destroy. But who are you to judge another? (Jas 4:12).

> and the prayer of faith will heal [*sōzō*] him who is sick, and the Lord will raise him up. If he has committed sins, he will be forgiven (Jas 5:15).

> let him know that he who turns a sinner from the error of his way will save [*sōzō*] a soul from death and will cover a multitude of sins (Jas 5:20).

At first glance, the uses in 1:21 and 5:20 seem to heavily imply eternal salvation. After all, what else would the salvation of the soul be?

The usage in 4:12 is somewhat ambiguous, although I'm inclined to say it's probably temporal. On my reading, the point is that we leave judgment to God. James certainly isn't talking here about us rendering eternal judgment. The idea, then, should be that we should even leave *temporal* judgment (the kind we render) to God, since He can save (temporally) or destroy (temporally). This isn't, of course, saying that God can't or doesn't eternally save or destroy. It's just to keep the passage focused on the actual context.

Against these, the usage in 5:15 is, for me, obviously temporal. Although some denominations use this verse to ground one of their sacraments, making it about eternal salvation, it's clearly about physical healing, a usage attested elsewhere in the Bible (cf. Mark 5:23; Luke 8:36; Acts 14:19, etc.).

Therefore, we might argue that the other uses are split, leaving us without clear guidance on how the word is used in James 2. However, we now need to revisit the phrase "salvation of the soul." Is that *really* about eternal salvation?

Salvation of the Soul in the LXX

Since James was steeped in the Greek Old Testament (the LXX), it's crucial to see what "save the soul" meant there. This lets us test whether James's phrase would naturally be read as "save from hell" or "preserve life from danger." There are 9 clear references to the salvation of the soul in the LXX. If you want to confirm this yourself and don't read Greek, you can go to blueletterbible.com and search for G4982 and G5590.

If you then read through the OT passages, you'll find that while the words *sōzō* and *psychē* (soul/life) occur together in 20 verses, only 9 of those are used in the phrase "save your soul." The other 11 just have the words in the same verse, though not connected in the phrase we're looking for. For example, here's the Greek (LXX) text of Jer. 39:18 (which, for reasons I won't go into in this post, is Jer. 46:18 in the LXX), along with Brenton's translation of the passage:

> For I will surely save thee, and thou shalt by no means fall by the sword; and thou shalt find thy life, because thou didst trust in me, saith the Lord (Jer 39:18; LXX Jer 46:18 Brenton).

This passage is helpful just because it shows a clear example in which salvation (*sōzō*) isn't salvation from hell. But it doesn't help us with the phrase "save your soul." With that said, here's all 9 passages in which we *do* find the phrase (all Brenton):

> And it came to pass when they brought them out, that they said, Save [*sōzō*] thine own life [*psychē*] by all means; look not round to that which is behind, nor stay in all the country round about, escape to the mountain, lest perhaps thou be overtaken together with them (Gen 19:17).

> And Jacob called the name of that place, the Face of God; for, [said he,] I have seen God face to face, and my life [*psychē*] was preserved [*sōzō*] (Gen 32:30; LXX: Gen 32:31).

> And it came to pass in that night, that Saul sent messengers to the house of David to watch him, in order to slay him in the morning; and Melchol David's wife told him, saying, Unless thou save [*sōzō*] thy life [*psychē*] this night, to-morrow thou shalt be slain (1 Sam 19:11)

> Deliver [*sōzō*] my soul (*psychē*), that it may not go to destruction, and my life shall see the light (Job 33:28).

> I will exult and be glad in thy mercy: for thou hast looked upon mine affliction; thou hast saved [*sōzō*] my soul [*psychē*] from distresses (Ps 31:7; LXX: Ps 30:8).

> He shall spare the poor and needy, and shall deliver [*sōzō*] the souls [*psychē*] of the needy (Ps 72:13; LXX: Ps 71:31).

> Flee ye, and save [*sōzō*] your lives [*psyche*], and ye shall be as a wild ass in the desert (Jer 48:6; LXX: Jer 31:6).

> And flight shall perish from the runner, and the strong shall not hold fast his strength, and the warrior

shall not save [*sōzō*] his life [*psychē*]: (Amos 2:14)

and the archer shall not withstand, and he that is swift of foot shall in no wise escape; and the horseman shall not save [*sōzō*] his life [*psychē*] (Amos 2:15)

It should be incredibly obvious that *all* of these refer to the deliverance of one's temporal life from a threat against it. The only borderline case is Job 33:28, but the Hebrew parallelism, to say nothing of the larger theme of the book, makes it plain that Elihu is sharing the speech of an already righteous man seeking restoration from struggles in this life, even if and when those struggles are the direct result of sin.

Here's the takeaway: if the phrase "save [the] soul" always refers to temporal salvation of the life in the Old Testament, doesn't it make sense that James is using it the same way? Put differently, is there anything in James that suggests that he is using the phrase *differently* than it is found everywhere else in Scripture? Or still another question: suppose that every instance of "save [the] soul" in the OT clearly referred to salvation from hell—wouldn't that be *strong* evidence that James was using it in just that way, also? But if so, doesn't that mean that the OT usage is *strong* evidence that James means it as temporal salvation?

Sōzō in James, Revisited

We should conclude, then, that James 1:21, 5:15, and 5:20 *unambiguously* refer to temporal salvation, and that 4:12 *probably* refers to temporal salvation. Therefore, we should take this as *strong* evidence that, shy of strong reasons in James 2 itself to think that salvation from hell is in view, we should assume he is using the word in the same sense. Namely, salvation James 2 is almost certainly temporal salvation of the soul from a danger to this life.

What about "Salvation" in the OT more generally?

I think the data above is more than enough to show that the prima facie case for James 2 having temporal salvation in view is prohibitively strong. But I think there's one more important piece of evidence we should consider, which is how "salvation" is used in the OT more generally. The reason this is important is that our modern ears hear, "Can faith save him?" and we simply find it absurd to think that this is about anything other than salvation from hell. In other words, our starting assumption is that "save" refers to salvation from hell unless proved otherwise. But notice that this assumption is just that—an assumption. It's one largely driven by our theology and tradition rather than the text itself. I want to try to show that James's readers would have thought that *our* assumption is the absurd one, that they held the *opposite* assumption. For them, salvation was always temporal unless there was good reason to think otherwise.

To give you a basic statistic, there are 271 basic uses of the word *sōzō* in the OT, plus another 107 occurrences of the noun "salvation" (*sōteria*), and finally another 22 instances of the word "savior" (*sōtēr*). I'm not going to do an analysis of all 300 occurrences. For now, I'll say that a very preliminary analysis suggests to me that less than a third of all uses of "save" and its cognates in the OT could even possibly refer to salvation from hell. In fact, the strongest candidates for such a reading (in my initial review) left me with only about 4% of the total, and even *those* represent my desire to be *extremely* charitable to the "salvation from hell" crowd. I can quite plausibly, and maybe preferably, argue that *all* of these are talking about temporal salvation! (For those who want to review—and again, this was only based on an initial and quick review, so I might change even these in a later assessment—cf. Ps 30:3; 51:14; 79:9; 119:155; Prov 15:24; Job 13:16; Isa 25:9; 45:17; Jer 4:14; 23:6; Joel 2:32; and Hab 3:13.)

The point is that the *vast* majority of the times that *sōzō* is used in the OT, it refers to temporal, not eternal, salvation. But before we wrap up this already long post, let me give you nine more specific data points, as the paragraph above is really little more than my rough interpretation of the data. Rather than trying to say anything about the 300 uses of *sōzō* (and cognates) in the OT, let me look at the nine uses of *sōzō* in Proverbs. The reason is that James is widely regarded as something like the wisdom literature of the New Testament. Therefore, the use of *sōzō* in Proverbs is probably instructive as to how James and his readers would have been inclined to read the word. Same as above, here are the verses (in Brenton's translation):

[My] son, do what I command thee, and deliver [*sōzō*] thyself; for on thy friend's account thou art come into the power of evil [men]: faint not, but stir up even thy friend for whom thou art become surety. Give not sleep to thine eyes, nor slumber with thine eyelids; that thou mayest deliver [*sōzō*] thyself as a doe out of the toils, and as a bird out of a snare (Prov 6:3-5).

When the storm passes by, the ungodly vanishes away; but the righteous turns aside and escapes [*sōzō*] for ever (Prov 10:25).

If the righteous scarcely be saved [*sōzō*], where shall the ungodly and the sinner appear? (Prov 11:31).

The thoughts of the wise are ways of life, that he may turn aside and escape [*sōzō*] from hell. A receiver of bribes destroys himself; but he that hates the receiving of bribes is safe [*sōzō*] (Prov 15:24, 27).

Every one who hates [his] poor brother shall also be far from friendship. Good understanding will draw near to them that know it, and a sensible man will find it. He that does much harm perfects mischief; and he that uses provoking words shall not escape [*sōzō*] (Prov 19:7).

He that trusts to a bold heart, such an one is a fool: but he that walks in wisdom shall be safe [*sōzō*] (Prov 28:26).

[they] fearing and reverencing men [unreasonably] have been overthrown, but he that trusts in the Lord shall rejoice. Ungodliness causes a man to stumble: but he that trusts in his master shall be safe [*sōzō*] (Prov 29:25).

I think it is self-evident, as you read through these, that the only plausible candidate for eternal salvation is Prov 15:24, and this is only because "from hell" is used. But it doesn't take much study to learn that "hell" in the OT typically just refers to the grave, death, or destruction. We might also consider Prov 10:25 something of a border case due to the addition of "for ever." But insofar as the LXX is trying to capture the idea of the Hebrew text, I don't think this is a serious candidate for eternal salvation. The KJV rendering of Prov 10:25 is "As the whirlwind passeth, so *is* the wicked no *more*: but the righteous *is* an everlasting foundation." I don't think we should argue that believers are a "foundation" in the sense of "going to heaven."

But even if we are generous and count *both* of these as salvation from hell (and I dispute both), then that means two of nine occurrences in Proverbs, or 22%—which is consistent with the less than one third I found in my broader study—refers to eternal salvation. And, importantly, *both* of those contain strong linguistic flags ("from hell," "forever," respectively) that eternity might be in view!

Summary

So what can we conclude from this survey of the actual textual data of how *sōzō* and its cognates are used in the Old Testament, which would have been James's own textual tradition? We've seen:

The word "save" can lexically refer to rescue from some temporal danger (a meaning it *definitely* carries at least once in James itself) or salvation from hell;

The two strongest candidates for salvation from hell in James itself (1:21 and 5:20) are based on a phrase ("save the soul") that is *exclusively* used in the OT to refer to temporal deliverance of the physical life from some danger, suggesting James would use it the same way; and

The broader use of "save" and cognates in the OT strongly suggest that salvation from eternal hell is a minority reading (from 0% to as much as 30% of uses), and that such a meaning—if it exists at all—is marked with explicit linguistic flags to signal as such. Those flags, however, do not exist in James 2.

Conclusion

In conclusion, then, we are on *very* strong grounds to read James 2:14 as referring to salvation from temporal danger, *not* to salvation from eternal Hell.

In light of this, I want to point to Jas 2:14 as a great illustration of why *semper reformanda* (Always reforming!) remains an important and powerful truth. As far as I can tell, the *reason* we tend to read this verse as if it's about salvation from Hell is almost entirely driven by tradition. We've simply not thought to ask if that's the view that James had in mind. We Protestants and evangelicals should remember that we are reading this verse downstream from Catholic soteriology and American revivalism. We're *still* learning to reread the text as it would have been read in the first century. It's hard to remove our Augustinian glasses, but this is one case I think we can see (pun intended) why such a move is necessary!

Matthew 24:13

Daniel Weierbach

"Many try to take that text and try to get out of it by saying Jesus right is talking about enduring to the end of the Tribulation. If you live through the whole Tribulation, then your body will be saved. That's not the context. The context there is on the heels...of Jesus warning in verses 9, 10, 11 and 12 that many will fall away from the faith and they'll be seduced by false Christ and false prophets." ~Joe Schimmel

Introduction

Matthew 24:13 is one of those verses where some people believe they see a necessity to endure in good works and faith in order to keep eternal life. Unfortunately, this view overlooks the dozens of verses that clearly explain eternal life is given by grace, through faith, not by works. Also, if endurance were a necessary condition for keeping eternal life, it would be considered a *debt*, giving man a reason to boast, nullifying grace (cf. Rom 4:4).

So why do some people believe Matt 24:13 teaches conditional security (i.e., that you can lose your salvation)? First, some believe the word *saved* has only one definition, namely, to escape hell and go to heaven. And second, because people have forgotten the Jewish perspective of the Scriptures.

Understanding How "Salvation" Is Used

The word *saved*, or *sōzō* in the Greek, has multiple definitions: to rescue from natural dangers and afflictions, save from physical death, keep from harm, bring out safely, save from disease, to guard or preserve, and to keep from eternal death.[1] It does not only refer to eternal salvation. With a word that carries so many definitions, we must determine which definition is most appropriate in Matt 24:13 based on the context.

Approaching Matthew 24

The immediate context begins in Matt 24:1, when the disciples discuss the buildings of the Temple. It is here that Jesus makes a very poignant statement,

> "I say to you, not one stone shall be left here upon another, that shall not be thrown down"[2] (Matt 24:2)

Jesus states those Temple buildings will be utterly destroyed. To this pronouncement, the disciples ask three specific questions:

1) When will these things be?
2) What will be the sign of Your coming?
3) What will be the sign of the end of the age?

Therefore, the *salvation* which Jesus speaks about in v 13 is directly related to one of these questions.

Jesus' reply contains the conjunctive adverb *then* in vv 9, 10, 11, and 14:

> "Then they will deliver you up to tribulation and kill you, and you will be hated by all nations for My name's sake. And then many will be offended, will betray one another, and will hate one another. Then many false prophets will rise up and deceive many...

---

[1] Bauer, Walter. *A Greek-English Lexicon of the New Testament and Other Early Christian Literature* (p. 982). University of Chicago Press. Kindle Edition.
[2] NKJV is used throughout

And this gospel of the kingdom will be preached in all the world as a witness to all the nations, and then the end will come" (emphasis added).

That reveals a chronological order to these events. To understand the full chronology, we must go back to v 4.

The Beginning of Sorrows

Beginning in v 4, Jesus states there will be: deception, false Messiahs will rise, wars, rumors of wars, kingdom divisions, and famines, pestilences, and earthquakes in various places. Jesus says, "these are the beginning of sorrows."[3] It is after these events occur that the first *then* appears. This reveals that the Jews will be hated and betrayed, false prophets will deceive many, lawlessness will abound, and love will grow cold *after* the events of Matt 24:4-8.

After understanding the order of events in vv 4-12, we must ask what the *end* is and, out of the range of meanings for *sōzō*, what *saved* means in that context.

In v 14, Jesus states the "gospel of the kingdom will be preached to all the world as a witness to all the nations," and "then the end will come." The *end* in Matt 24:13 and 14 must be understood in light of the original question, "What will be the sign of the *end* of the age?" Of which Jesus states it will not occur until after the "beginning of sorrows."[4]

The "end of the age" will occur at the completion of the Tribulation Period, otherwise known as the Seventieth Week of Daniel.[5] The end of that age will see the establishment of the Messianic Kingdom, which will bring in the age of everlasting righteousness.[6] So, the "end of the age" is understood as the end of the Tribulation Period. Therefore, those who "endure to the end" are the Jewish remnant alive *during that time period*. This is further supported by v 15 when Jesus refers to Dan 12:11 regarding the abomination of desolation being set up in the Temple area.

---

[3] Matthew 24:8
[4] Matthew 24:6, 8
[5] Daniel 9:27
[6] Daniel 9:24

Saved from What?

Those who "endure to the end" of the Tribulation period will be saved. But saved in what sense? This is where a Jewish perspective provides tremendous clarity.

When Jesus speaks of the "gospel of the kingdom" being preached, He does not mean the gospel that many Christians think of today. Rather, He is referring to the gospel of the Messianic Kingdom. Due to the Jews committing the unpardonable sin, Jesus' offer to establish His Kingdom was rescinded and postponed until a later time, when the Jewish people would acknowledge Him as their Messiah. Once that happens, as Jesus promises in Matt 23:39, He will return, rescue Israel, and set up His Kingdom on earth.

Staying in the immediate context of Matthew 24, we see God's divine deliverance (e.g., "be saved"), based upon the believing Jewish remnant fleeing Jerusalem, according to Matt 24:15-22. This remnant will be protected by God in an area known as the wilderness,[7] and as Zech 13:9 says, "they shall call on my name and I will hear them." It is at that time that Jesus Christ will physically return, *saving* the faithful remnant from physical death, and setting up His Messianic Kingdom, ushering in the new age.

Conclusion

So, what does Jesus mean when He says, "he who endures to the end shall be saved"? The Lord is not making endurance a condition of eternal salvation. He means that the Jewish believers who flee Jerusalem when the Antichrist sets up the abomination of desolation will be physically spared from his terror and divinely rescued by the return of Messiah as a conquering King. This is clear based on the immediate context, the three original questions from the disciples regarding the "end of the age," and understanding the Jewish perspective of the Messianic Kingdom.

---

[7] Revelation 12:14

Revelation 3:5

Luke Morrison

"Yes, you're Christians now, but if you do this, this, and this in terms of belief and behavior, well, your name can be erased from the Lamb's book of eternal life." ~Ben Witherington III

Introduction

This verse has caused an unknown amount of consternation to many Biblical interpreters. In the verse, we read, "The one who conquers will be clothed thus in white garments, and I will never blot his name out of the book of life…." (Rev 3:5 ESV). I believe we can learn more about this means by looking at what Christ said in the first verse of the chapter. Remember, context is king in all Bible interpretations.

The Context in Sardis

In v 1, we read that the church in Sardis had a reputation for being alive, but it was dead. A dead church may very well have some unbelievers in it claiming salvation, but it may also have many believers who are more worldly than heavenly. I believe Sardis was full of believers, many of whom were not living for the Lord. I say this because vv 2 and 3 encourage the church to "wake up and strengthen what remains" and "remember…what you received and heard. Keep it, and repent." These phrases indicate the church was full of people who had believed in Jesus but were not living that life.

It seems that many believed but then drifted into worldly living, which may have attracted people to the church, making it look alive while it was dead. Or maybe the church members had suffered persecution and began to act as if they were not Christian to save their lives. Or perhaps they feared persecution and did not actively live out their faith. From commentaries discussing the historical aspect of this church, one finds that persecutions were inflicted, including names being blotted from "the town registers."[1]

Paige Patterson notes that another curse said, "may the Nazarenes and the Minim [Ebionites]...be blotted out of the book of life."[2] That could have caused this concern. The church at Sardis had genuine concern about being blotted from books within the community, and they may have begun to act in a manner that caused them not to live as believers should. If this is correct, the statement "I will never blot his name out from the Book of Life" promises believers that their names are secure in the Book of Life.

A Word of Encouragement

When this historical backdrop is understood, Jesus' statement becomes an *encouragement* rather than a *threat*. That is because the Lord promises and encourages believers to become overcomers rather than hiding or allowing worldly influence into their lives. He is saying, "As one of mine, even though the community may remove you from their roles, I will never do that to you." Also, Christ is saying that if they stay faithful, even though they are hated and looked down on here and possibly spit on and abused as He was, they will have pure white robes in eternity.

As the book of Revelation further expresses about being clothed in white, Charlie Bing argues that this is the reward for faithful living (cf. Rev 19:8, 14).[3] The more faithful and committed a believer is, the more special rewards Christ will give them in the presence of the Father, but all believers will keep their names in the Book of Life.

---

[1] Paige Patterson, *Revelation*, vol. 39, *The New American Commentary*, ed. E. Ray Clendenen, (Nashville, TN: B&H, 2012), 123.
[2] Patterson, *Revelation*, 123.
[3] Charles C. Bing, *Grace, Salvation, and Discipleship: How to Understand Some Difficult Bible Passages* (Brenham, TX: Lucid Books, 2015), 245.

A Figure of Speech

Bing argues that this statement means exactly what it says: their names will not be blotted out because it is an emphatic expression stating they will never be removed.[4] It assures the believers that they are in the book and will not be blotted out. Jesus's statement is a figure of speech known as a litotes, a form of understatement that ironically expresses the affirmative by negating the contrary. For example, if you say, "It's not the best weather today," during a hurricane, you mean the weather is horrible. Or if you say, "This cake is not that bad," you mean the cake is good. That kind of ironic understatement is what is happening in Rev 3:5.

When Christ says that believers will not have their names blotted out of the Book of Life, He means He will keep their names in it. As Dillow explains: "The negative idea is not central. Rather, the interpreter must focus on the positive idea to which the negative refers… when the Lord says, "*I will not blot his name out*," He is not implying that there is such a possibility, but He is saying emphatically that He will keep his name in the book."[5]

It is because of this figure of speech, as well as many verses throughout Scripture, that this verse is not a threat but a promise. Patterson is correct when he said viewing this verse as a promise and not a threat, "and that is certainly the way a first-century reader would have read it —Then verses like these do nothing to suggest the possibility of forfeiting salvation once and for all received."[6]

Conclusion

Scripture repeatedly promises that the believer in Jesus Christ has eternal life that cannot be lost. Too many interpreters want to impose a condition of "works" across Scripture: works for us to prove, keep, or earn our eternal life. Yet, that teaching leads to believers' having doubts and insecurities about their salvation because we can never know if we have overcome enough, worked hard enough, or lived well enough to keep eternal life. That is why this verse is so comforting.

---

[4] Ibid.
[5] Joseph C. Dillow, *Final Destiny: The Future Reign of the Servant Kings, 4th Edition* (Houston, TX: Grace Theology Press, 2018), 687.
[6] Patterson, *Revelation*, 124.

Jesus said He will *never* blot out a believer's name from the Book of Life. You can take this promise to the bank and know it is true.

The Book of Life and Revelation 3:5

Marty Cauley

"They say, 'Oh, my name's in the book of life. It'll be there forever.' Is Jesus telling a lie here? Is He making an empty threat? If you overcome, your name will never be erased from the Book of Life. What if you don't overcome?" ~Zac Poonen

Introduction

The promise that overcomers will not have their names blotted out of the Book of Life in Rev 3:5 must be interpreted harmoniously with the announcement in Rev 20:15 that anyone whose name is not found there will be cast into the Lake of Fire.

Those who reject eternal security condition salvation from the Lake of Fire on being an overcomer in the experiential sense of the word.

Those who think salvation can be forfeited assert that believers who do not overcome lose eternal life, have their names erased, and are condemned to Hell.

Those who believe works must prove salvation think that believers who do not overcome never had their names written in the Book of Life.

Eternal security advocates have proposed several alternative interpretations of the Book of Life.

Not all believers overcome in the sense described in Revelation 2–3. This raises the question of whether their names are erased. Disagreement among eternal security advocates on this issue adds further complexity to the debate, underscoring the need for further exploration. Several popular options are available.

Option 1: A Single Book of Life

Some eternal security advocates propose only one Book of Life. One variation of this *single-book hypothesis* states that names cannot be erased. Revelation 3:5 is not a warning that non-overcomers will have their names erased but a litotes promising that the Lord will honor the names of overcomers.

Litotes are common in Johannine literature. John uses approximately sixty formal litotes in his writings. A *formal litotes* is an understatement that implicitly indicates the opposite by using explicit negation. He also adds functional litotes. A *functional litotes* is an understatement that implicitly indicates the opposite through implicit negation. Many interpreters and even some conditionalists recognize that not having one's name blotted out in Rev 3:5 is a litotes, an understatement affirming the opposite will occur. Overcomers will be rewarded with having their names *honored*. The inverse of a litotes is not necessarily implied. Indeed, sometimes an inversion is perversion. Therefore, some eternal security advocates insist that the inverse of this litotes is not applicable. They insist that unfaithful believers will not have their names erased, just not honored.

Option 2: Multiple Books

On the other hand, some believers in eternal security propose the possibility of unfaithful believers having their names erased *in terms of rewards*.

One suggestion offered is a *multiple-book hypothesis*. According to this theory, there are multiple books of life. The complexity of the Biblical data favors multiple books. The OT pictures a Book of Physical Life (cf. Exod 32:32, Ps 69:28), while Revelation discusses the Lamb's Book of Life (cf. Rev 21:27) as possibly distinct from the Book of Life. Additionally, eternal life is frequently depicted in the NT and Revelation as having both salvation and reward dimensions. So, posing two separate books for each aspect of eternal life is certainly within the realm of reason. A passage such as Rev 3:5 could be talking about a rewards-related Book of Life (about rewards within the kingdom), while a passage such as Rev 20:15 could be talking about a salvation-related Book of Life (about entrance into the kingdom). Believers could have their names removed from the former (in terms of rewards) but not from the latter (in terms of salvation from the Lake of Fire). Unfaithful believers might lose their potential qualification to rule in the kingdom, but they cannot lose their right to dwell within the kingdom.

Additionally, the Book of Life seems to have a duality of salvation and rewards in some passages. In short, the Book of Life is used in four capacities. (1) *Book of earthly citizenship*: it may refer to citizenship on Earth (secular usage). (2) *Book of earthly life*: it may refer to life on Earth—(Exod 32:32-33; Ps 69:28a; 139:16). (3) *Book of rewards-related life*: it may refer to life in the Heavenly Jerusalem—(Ps 69:28b; Isa 4:3-4; cf. Rev 3:5b; 3:12; 21:27; 22:19?); Luke 10:20 (secondarily?); Phil 3:20 (primarily); Heb 12:23; Rev 3:5b (primarily), 13:8 (primarily?); 17:8 (secondarily?); 20:12, 15 (secondarily?); 21:27 (primarily). (4) *Book of soteriological life*: it may refer to life in heaven—Dan 12:1-2; Luke 10:20 (dualistically); Phil 3:20 (dualistically); 4:3 (dualistically?); Rev 3:5b (dualistically); 13:8 (dualistically?); 17:8 (dualistically?); 20:12-15 (dualistically?); 21:27 (dualistically).

Option 3: Composite Book

Accordingly, some eternal security advocates pose a *composite-book hypothesis*—a singular book of life with a rewards-related entry to the right of each name, perhaps a crown denoting whether the believer is an overcomer. Faithful believers who overcome and thus qualify to be kingdom rulers might have a crown beside their name. One possibility is that the names of believers are written before the foundation of the world and are thus permanent and cannot be erased, but the crown beside their name can be erased if they fail to overcome. If so, the Book of Life has permanent entries for salvation and potentially erasable notations for rewards.

Option 4: Book of Life Spreadsheet

An even more advanced approach is to pose a *Book of Life Spreadsheet*. For instance, this model may suggest that this spreadsheet has the names of believers (Rev 20:15) written in its first column from the foundation of the world (Rev 17:8), which suggests that their names are permanently recorded within it and cannot be erased. Nevertheless, their names may be erased in some secondary capacity (Rev 3:5). Thus, the *names* of everyone who would ever believe in Christ for eternal life as a free gift have been recorded permanently from the foundation of the world in the first column. They have other columns besides their names.

Check marks for overcomers' rewards could have been recorded from the foundation of the world in the final column. The initial and final columns are static. The intervening columns are marked during the course of time. The second column could be a record of physical life. The third column could be a record of salvific life. This would be a dynamic-static column in that once a check mark is entered in this column (at the inception of regeneration), that check mark cannot be erased. The next column could be a record of presumptive rewards-related life.

Revelation 3:5 provides an example regarding presumptive rewards. Jesus distinguishes between potential and actual rewards when He warns: "Hold fast what you have, in order that no one take your crown" (Rev 3:11). Not having one's reward status erased is the promise if you are faithful to the end. Believers still alive on Earth have the potential to earn the crown of life. At the point of death, they will no longer have the potential to earn this reward. At that point, they either qualify to actualize that potential or they do not. During their lives, believers are presumed to have their names recorded as qualifying for crowns, but this rewards-related status can be forfeited if, at the Bema, they are found to be unfaithful. Their name's check mark can be erased from this column. If so, their potential to rule the kingdom will go unrealized. They will have forfeited that potential reward. If so, they will not qualify for the Crown of Life (cf. Jas 1:12; Rev 2:10) nor the Tree of Life (Rev 22:14,19). Of course, they will still be able to drink from the Water of Life outside the City since the water is freely available to all believers (Rev 22:17).

Ephesians 1:13-14

Kenneth McClure

"In Greek, a seal is often a stamp, a seal of approval, a seal that a king puts on something that it belongs to him. And seals can be broken. Stamps can be effaced."
~Matthew Pinson

Introduction

Ephesians 1:13-14 is a powerful passage that provides insight into the concept of "once saved, always saved" and the idea of eternal security for believers. In these verses, the apostle Paul writes to the Ephesian church, highlighting the role of the Holy Spirit in sealing believers as a guarantee of their inheritance until the redemption of God's possession. In this context, the term "sealed" holds significant theological implications that support the doctrine of eternal security.

In Ephesians 1, Paul writes,

> **And you also were included in Christ when you heard the message of truth, the gospel of your salvation. When you believed, you were marked in him with a seal, the promised Holy Spirit, who is a deposit guaranteeing our inheritance until the redemption of those who are God's possession—to the praise of his glory (Eph 1:13-14).**

This passage emphasizes the role of the Holy Spirit as a seal upon believers, signifying their identity as God's chosen and marking them as secure in their salvation.

What Does It Mean to Be Sealed?

The term "sealed" carries several important connotations that support the idea of once saved, always saved.

First and foremost, a seal serves as a mark of ownership and authenticity. In ancient times, a seal was used to mark a document or object as belonging to a particular individual or entity. Similarly, the Holy Spirit's seal upon believers signifies that they belong to God and are His cherished possession. This seal of ownership underscores the security and permanence of believers' salvation, as they are eternally bound to God through the work of the Holy Spirit.

Second, a seal also serves as a guarantee or pledge of something to come. In Eph 1:13-14, the Holy Spirit is described as a deposit guaranteeing our inheritance until the redemption of God's possession. This language conveys the idea that the presence of the Holy Spirit in the life of a believer is a down payment or assurance of the future fulfillment of God's promises. Just as a seal secures and guarantees the contents of a document or package, the Holy Spirit's seal upon believers ensures the fulfillment of God's redemptive plan and the ultimate salvation of His people.

Third, the concept of being sealed by the Holy Spirit also highlights the idea of divine protection and preservation. A seal serves as a form of protection, safeguarding the contents it encloses from tampering or harm. Similarly, the Holy Spirit's seal upon believers signifies God's protection and preservation of His chosen ones, ensuring they are kept safe and secure in their relationship with Him. This divine seal of protection reinforces the assurance of believers' eternal security and underscores the faithfulness and power of God to keep His promises.

Conclusion

In conclusion, Eph 1:13-14 provides a rich theological foundation for the doctrine of eternal security and the concept of "once saved, always saved." The term "sealed" in this passage signifies believers' identity as God's chosen possession, the guarantee of their inheritance, and the divine protection and preservation of their salvation. The Holy Spirit's seal serves as a mark of ownership, a pledge of future fulfillment, and a symbol of God's faithfulness and power. Ultimately, the sealing of believers by the Holy Spirit affirms the eternal security of their salvation and the unshakable promise of God to keep and preserve His people until the day of redemption.

A Dual Seal in Ephesians 1:13-14

Marty Cauley

"So we have been sealed with the Holy Spirit, meaning we have received the Holy Spirit as an inheritance, as a deposit on what is to come." ~Michael Brown

Introduction

Advocates for eternal security interpret Eph 1:13-14 as related to salvation, thus unconditionally assuring those who have believed that they will reach Heaven. Conditionalists counter that eternal security is not intended in that passage. Advocates of eternal rewards can allow both perspectives with a dualism of salvation and rewards. For example, one dualist option is to propose that the seal is a promise of eternal security, while the earnest is a promise of conditional rewards possibility. Another dualistic option perceives both the sealing and earnest as complementary salvation and rewards vantage points.

Believers Are Marked in Two Ways

Believers are marked in two ways—in terms of salvation as family members and in terms of rewards as potential heirs of the kingdom. Realizing this potential requires that they fulfill certain conditions. Just as we were chosen for salvation in Eph 1:4 because of our punctiliar saving faith, we were marked/sealed/identified for rewards in Eph 1:13 as potential heirs as a result of having believed.

Immersion in the Spirit is referred to as a sealing, which is necessarily salvific and applies to all believers. Since immersion in the Spirit is the means by which we are made part of the body of Christ at regeneration and become new creatures in Christ (cf. 2 Cor 5:17), the sealing with the Spirit is a salvific event. However, the sealing may be for rewards, namely, that we might receive an inheritance and rewards-redemption.

Where salvation is concerned, this sealing has a positional function in making us a new person. It is used in the soteriological connection with us becoming a new man/creation in Christ and shows God's salvation-related approval regarding His salvation-related ownership. This sealing relates to salvation in that it applies to all believers at the point of faith. As Paul notes in Colossians, the sister epistle to Ephesians, all believers are initially qualified for this inheritance (Col 1:12).

However, exhortation is provided for the realization of the inheritance as a reward (Col 3:24). Likewise, Paul warns believers to live in a godly way since ungodly behavior disqualifies them from the realization of the kingdom inheritance (Eph 5:5). The inheritance of the kingdom is dualistic in that it is presumptively granted to all believers originally but only realized by faithful believers eschatologically.

Can Believers Lose the Spirit?

If believers forfeit this inheritance, do they lose the Spirit?

In the parable of the ten virgins (Matt 25:1-13), we see that unfaithful believers can lose the Holy Spirit in the sense of not having the spiritual reserves necessary to be qualified to participate in the rewards of the marriage festivities. All church-age believers are *indwelt* by the Spirit (in their spirits), but they are not all *filled* with the Spirit (in their souls). Losing the filling of the Spirit can be pictured as losing the Spirit within the soul.

In Matt 25:1-13, the oil can run out, representing the lack of the filling of the Spirit in the soul. Likewise, believers can be temporally thrown away from Christ and cast away from Christ, like dried branches (John 15:6), representing a loss of rewards. Believers can be experientially severed from Christ (Gal 5:4). They can be cast into the outer darkness, away from Christ, in a rewards sense (Matt 8:12; 22:13; 25:30). Therefore, positing that believers can lose the Spirit in one sense but not the other is reasonable. Believers can lose the Spirit's empowerment for kingdom rulership (cf. 1 Sam 16:14; Ps 51:10).

Eternal security advocates can agree that all believers have the Spirit in a salvific sense, but not all believers have the Spirit in an experiential sense. This is but a hair's breadth away from acknowledging that unfaithful believers can lose the Holy Spirit in a rewards sense. Frankly, it only makes sense that unfaithful believers will lose out on intimacy with the Spirit and the empowerment that the Spirit could have provided otherwise. Intimacy with the Father and the Son is conditional. Surely, we must conclude that intimacy with the Spirit is also conditional (cf. Eph 4:30). We certainly know that the Spirit's empowerment is conditional. Therefore, typology would suggest that just as David feared losing the regal anointing of the Spirit, NT believers can lose the sealing of the Spirit as it relates to their having God's stamp of approval as being qualified to inherit the kingdom as kingdom rulers. Since the sealing pertains to being qualified to be in the running as a potential heir of the kingdom, those who fail the race must lose that regal aspect of the sealing. They could lose the Spirit as a rewards-based seal/earnest but not as a soteriological seal/pledge. It could be that the former is the exclusive intent of *arrabōn* here (a pledge, deposit, or down payment, Eph 1:14) and the latter is the exclusive intent elsewhere (2 Cor 1:22; 5:5) so that both sets of texts would be necessary to demonstrate the duality of *arrabōn*. Yet, since Paul intends a salvation–rewards duality for the seal in other singular texts (Rom 4:11; 2 Tim 2:19), posing a pledge-earnest duality for the *arrabōn* here is reasonable as well, especially considering the soteriological and rewards-based richness of its text and context.

A Joint Inheritance?

Considering the current hypothesis of duality in Eph 1:13-14, the richness of the text concerning the *inheritance* and *redemption* in v 14 needs to be re-examined. Paul is ambiguous. He is talking about *our* inheritance. But Paul does not specify if he is talking about *our* (believers') possession or *His* (God's) possession. Is Paul talking about the redemption of our possession, namely, our inheritance—thus *the redemption of our inheritance*, or is Paul talking about *the redemption of us as God's possession* (ultimately *as His inheritance*; cf. Eph 1:18)?

Duality suggests that Paul is masterfully using ambiguity to affirm both possibilities.

Paul affirms God's soteriological possession of us and our rewards-based inheritance of the kingdom. This possession is *ours and His*. A combined interpretive translation may be suggested: "Who is the guarantee of our inheritance until *the* redemption of *our joint* possession, to the praise of His glory" (TM). This interpretive translation captures Paul's thought better in conveying the implicit mutuality implied by the Greek duality.

Adopting this joint-inheritance perspective in Eph 1:14 allows us to perceive Paul as saying that the Holy Spirit is "the guarantee of our inheritance until the redemption of our joint possession" (TM). Understandably, therefore, Paul warns: "And do not grieve the Holy Spirit of God, by whom you were sealed for the day of redemption" (Eph 4:30). Then, a few verses later, Paul clarifies that what is at stake in grieving the Holy Spirit is the inheritance in the kingdom. "For this you know with certainty, that no immoral or impure person or covetous man, who is an idolater, has an inheritance in the kingdom of Christ and God" (Eph 5:5). The reward aspect of the inheritance is at stake (cf. Col 3:23). Receiving the full inheritance is conditioned on being filled with the Spirit, which is impossible if one is grieving the Spirit. Those believers who grieve the Holy Spirit lose intimacy with Him and empowerment from Him in this life and the next. Nevertheless, they do not lose the life imparted by the Spirit to their spirit. In that respect, they will always have the Spirit within them.

Romans 7

L. E. Brown

"There is nothing in any of Paul's other letters that sound even remotely like Romans 7 as a paradigm or even a common experience in the Christian life. For this reason alone, we ought to be very wary of those who think that Romans 7 is describing a typical struggle for a typical Christian as they try to work out the Christian life." ~Scot McKnight

Introduction

An experienced driver accelerates when she enters a freeway and brakes when entering a school zone. Instinctive habits developed by training and experience with little conscious thought. But those habits won't work if you put her in command of an orbiting spaceship. She'll discover she must accelerate to slow down but decelerate to speed up when orbiting Earth. Driving habits suitable for highways don't work in space.

Similarly, what works in natural life doesn't in the Christian life. Life in this world thrives on merit. From infancy we're taught that if we behave, work hard, do as we're told, we will "get ahead." The world teaches us we must work for everything.

The Christian life is different. The world's way of life often leads believers into defeat and spiritual despair. Striving for merit, playing by the rules, and self-effort cannot produce a fulfilling, Christ-honoring life. The way of the world leads to misery.

That's what Romans 7 is all about. The new life we receive when we believe in Jesus operates on different principles than the life received from our parents. This crucial chapter, within the context of chapters 5-8, explains how Christians live this new life. The preceding four chapters explain how sinners are justified before God.

Then, in Rom 5:1, we see a change in subject. "Therefore, having been justified by faith, we have peace with God through our Lord Jesus Christ." Two life paths lie before the believer (Rom 5:12-20). One leads to condemnation and death the other to life and freedom. The first path, considered in chap. 6, excuses the believer's sin. This is the way of death—not eternal condemnation but present alienation from God's fellowship and divine discipline that may result in premature death (Rom 6:23). Grace cannot be used to excuse sin!

The Way of Law-Keeping

The second path, treated in chap. 7, is the attempt to manage our sin by law-keeping. This path, too, leads to despair and defeat. Listen to the misery of a believer trying to cultivate the spiritual life by keeping the law: "I am carnal, sold under sin (v 14);" "What I am doing, I do not understand (v 15);" "What I will to do, that I do not practice (v 15)." "What I hate, that I do (v 15);" "I do what I will not to do (v 16);" "In me (that is, in my flesh) nothing good dwells (v 18);" "To will is present with me, but how to perform what is good I do not find (v 18);" "I find then a law, that evil is present with me, the one who wills to do good (v 21)." It got so bad for Paul that he cried out, "O wretched man that I am! Who will deliver me from this body of death? (v 24)." What a miserable way of life! Why would anyone direct new Christian believers to follow this path?

Some claim Paul wrote of the *unbeliever's* experience, but this is highly unlikely. After all, we find numerous statements about what Paul knew, intended, and desired while he tried to keep the law. What he wrote could not be true of unbelievers. Do unbelievers feel remorse for breaking God's law (v 15); declare that God's law is spiritual (v 14) and agree that it is good (v 16); wish to do good (vv 18, 21); and joyfully delight in God's law (v 22)? Also, note that "wretched man" is a term for believers in 2 Cor 4:16 and Eph 3:16.

Of course, not everyone agrees that Romans 7 is about a believer's experience in trying to keep the law. But this view has wide support throughout history. It was held by Augustine, Hilary, Ambrose, and Jerome in the early centuries. Gregory the Great and the Western church taught this view in the Medieval period. Later, the Reformers also taught this view; Luther and Calvin were proponents.[1] Barret, Bruce, Cranfield, Dunn, Morris, Nygren, and Packer are representative of many modern scholars who also hold this view.

Conclusion

Romans 5-7 presents two ways of conducting the Christian life. Both lead to failure. The first is the path of license; it excuses sin and disregards the consequences. Unchecked license leads to back to slavery, divine discipline, and even death. The second is the path of law-keeping, attempting to obey in one's own power. But this leads to defeat, depression, and despair.

What then, is the proper way for believers to live their new lives? Stay tuned for chapter eight!

---

[1] Stephen Voorwinde, "Romans 7—A History of Interpretation," *Vox Reformata* 2018, 78.

Romans 8:29-30

Marty Cauley

"Even when you look at the so called steps in these links in this golden chain, not any one step guarantees the next step." ~Joe Schimmel

Introduction

Advocates of eternal security typically take Rom 8:29-30 as a promise of unconditional security and object when conditionalists insert sanctification/perseverance as an unspoken sixth link into the chain of five links Paul presents. Yet, some believers in eternal security acknowledge that Rom 8:28, which introduces the chain, is conditional. Verse 29 begins with "for." When we look back at v 28 to see what the "for" is there for, the conditional implications flow from v 28 into v 29. Contextually, the golden chain only applies to those believers who love God, not all believers. Instead of an unconditional chain of salvation security, the passage describes a chain of rewards security.

Reading the Golden Chain in Light of Rewards

Even from a bird's eye view, a rewards perspective seems intuitive. Those believers who persevere are foreknown to do so and are thus assured of glory. God's election (Rom 8:33) is limited contextually to those elected according to God's purpose and who correspondingly love God (Rom 8:28) and who conform to the moral image of Jesus (Rom 8:29). The elect are those who persevere (Rom 8:25). This rewards-related glory is limited to those who persevere in their love for God and moral likeness of Christ.

The entire passage is an affirmation of rewards-related security for those believers who persevere.

The co-sufferings that co-heirs are enduring are to result in a co-glory with Christ (Rom 8:17b). This present day suffering will be followed eschatologically with the reward glory that is to be revealed to them as rewards-related heirs (Rom 8:18) who wait for rewards-related adoption as sons (Rom 8:23) by persevering (Rom 8:25). God causes all things to work together for the good of these rewardable heirs because they love Him and walk according to His purpose (Rom 8:28). For whom God foreknew would persevere, He also predestined to become conformed to the moral and rewards-related image of His Son, so that Jesus might be the firstborn among many rewardable brethren. And whom God predestined for rewards, these He also elected for rewards. And whom God elected, these He also justified in a rewards sense. And whom God justified, these He also glorified in a rewards sense (Rom 8:29-30). How will God not also graciously give us (i.e., the rewards-related heirs) all things? (Rom 8:32) Who will bring a charge against God's rewardable elect? God is the one who justifies them for rewards (Rom 8:33). Who is the one who condemns God's elect when it comes to their rewards? (Rom 8:34) Who will separate God's rewardable elect from the love of Christ? In all these things, the heirs overwhelmingly conquer through Him who loved them (Rom 8:37). Nothing will be able to separate rewards-related overcomers from the rewards-related love of God, which is in Christ Jesus our Lord (Rom 8:39).

Rewards and the Question of Confidence

The problem with this reward-centered interpretation is that rewards passages do not normally have such a high degree of confidence regarding the outcome. Yet the context of this passage stresses unconditional security and absolute assurance—an infallible rewards-related security. Believers must still meet the ongoing requirements for the final realization of their rewards, but God infallibly guarantees that the believers described by this passage will meet such requirements. The passage is a picture of unconditional ultimate realization for hyper-overcomers.

This is not a simple rewards-related chain but a hyper-rewards-related chain.

In Rom 8:37, the prefix *huper-* (*hyper*) in *hupernikao* has an intensifying effect. Paul is talking about *hyper-overcomers*. He says that God moves irresistibly in the lives of hyper-overcomers. Paul advocates unconditional security of rewards for this specific group. Not even hyper-overcomers can overturn God's election to the reward of co-glorification (Rom 8:33).

In both Rom 5:2 and Rom 8:29*ff*, hyper-overcomers have hyper-assurance. Their reward is 100% certain! To be sure, co-glorification is conditional. However, the ultimate realization of this conditional co-glorification is infallibly (and thus unconditionally and eternally) *secure and sure* for those overcomers who progress in their temporal experience to become hyper-overcomers. This irresistible result is unconditionally secure in terms of its ultimate completion.

An Effective Call to Rewards

God forechose to actualize a special group of overcomers for an irresistible process and conclusion that He would carry out. God did more than merely *foresee*; He *forechose* them. God's calling in this passage is not a mere *invitation* but an *effective call*. This call is a transition point from the general calling given to all saints to a point where some overcomers step through the door of lack of rewards-related rest into the state of rewards-related rest to become hyper-overcomers. This proleptic aorist serves as a door marking the punctiliar point in their lives when they become experientially assured of irresistibly reaching the final goal. The call is not issued at the end of their lives but at a particular punctiliar point during their lives. From this point in time, they can rest assured that they will reach New Jerusalem, the Reward City.

God does not accept charges against His rewards-relatedly *chosen ones* (His hyper-overcomers) who are already locked into His plans for them and which end in eternal Christlikeness. Those who enter this state are unconditionally assured of reaching their destination of Christlikeness as co-rulers with Christ. They have been predestined for this rewards-related destination.

They cannot escape their destined rewards. They can resist their destiny, but they cannot escape it since the end result is irresistible. They cannot escape their temporal suffering nor their ultimate rewards-related victory. God forechose those whom He foreknew would temporally enter His rest and pre-temporally and infallibly destined them for an eschatological realization of this rewards-related rest. God has sealed their rewards-related fate from within eternity past and for eternity future.

God's *elect* in Rom 8:33 are the rewards-relatedly chosen ones as described by the golden chain. They are hyper-overcomers. They heeded God's injunction: "Be diligent to enter that rest" (Heb 4:11). "Do your best to make your calling and election secure" (2 Pet 1:10; TM). They have entered the rewards-related rest and thereby made their rewards-related election secure. From that point onward, they can be sure of the outcome of being rewarded. Their sufferings cannot separate them from this irresistible conclusion.

Since God causes all things to work together for the good of hyper-overcomers, God will do whatever it takes to ensure they reach their reward-home in glory. Hyper-overcomers get hyper-divine enablement to ensure, in conjunction with the other tools in God's rewards-related toolbox, that they endure in the end, if not to the end. But this passage is limited to those believers who hyper-overcome. They persevere because they are called. In terms of temporal sequence, they are called before they have persevered to the end. They are called when they temporally enter the subjective rest of rewards-related assurance, ensuring their eschatological objective—rewards-related rest. Thus, their calling ensures their perseverance. And they know it! They have complete assurance concerning their rewards!

Conclusion

All believers can initially qualify for realizing this golden chain of rewards. Some believers will forfeit that potential. God may swear in His wrath that they will not enter His rest. From that point in time, entering God's rewards-related rest becomes impossible (cf. Hebrews 3-4). On the other hand, some faithful believers will appropriate this rest. God foreknew which believers would do so and forechose to call them effectively within this chain of events, thereby ensuring their ultimate success.

SECTION 3

More Reasons for Eternal Security

Sola Fide: Professed by Most, Truly Believed by Few

Vincenzo Russo

> "Justification by faith does not mean that there is a locked door behind us. Justification means that people have been launched into the kingdom of God, and they are now called to follow Jesus. If they choose to walk away from Jesus, it is because their faith has been broken, has collapsed, that they've chosen to walk away." ~Scot McKnight

Introduction

For centuries, the debate over salvation has been the defining divide between Roman Catholics and Protestants. Protestants have historically criticized the Catholic Church for teaching what they perceive as salvation by works, contrasting it with their rallying cry of salvation by grace alone, through faith alone. This doctrinal chasm was cemented during the Reformation, with Martin Luther famously declaring *sola fide* as the heart of the gospel. Yet, a closer look reveals a subtler issue at play. Many Protestants, particularly evangelicals and Reformed believers, affirm the oft-quoted phrase attributed to John Calvin: "We are saved by faith alone, but the faith that saves is never alone."

This qualification introduces works as evidence of salvation, echoing a process-oriented view that aligns more closely with Roman Catholic theology than is often recognized. A closer examination of the basics of soteriology held by Roman Catholics, Calvinists, and Arminians reveals significant common ground. All three traditions affirm that salvation is by God's grace and view it as a process rather than a one-time event. Furthermore, the emphasis Calvinists and Arminians place on perseverance and good works aligns them closer to Catholic theology than they may realize.

Therefore, the exploration undertaken here will challenge whether such views genuinely uphold the principle of *sola fide*, contrasting them with the distinct perspective of Free Grace theology, which fully embraces salvation as a one-time act of faith without conditions.

Salvation is All of Grace

Catholics, Calvinists, and Arminians all uphold the foundational truth that salvation begins and ends with God's grace. While each tradition articulates this differently, the central affirmation remains the same: humanity cannot save itself.

Roman Catholic Church

The Catholic Church unequivocally teaches that salvation is a gift of grace. The Council of Trent declared:

> If anyone says that man can be justified before God by his own works, whether done by his own natural powers or by the teaching of the law, without divine grace through Jesus Christ: let him be anathema (*Council of Trent*, Session 6, Canon 1).

In Catholic theology, human effort plays no role in initiating justification. Instead, grace is freely given, especially through the sacraments. Works, far from earning salvation, are the fruits of grace working in the believer.

Calvinism

Calvinism also places God's grace at the forefront. The Westminster Confession of Faith teaches:

> Faith, thus receiving and resting on Christ and His righteousness, is the alone instrument of justification;

yet it is not alone in the person justified, but is ever accompanied with all other saving graces, and is no dead faith, but worketh by love (WCF, XI.2)

Justification is entirely a work of God (monergism), and good works are evidence of true faith, not a means of earning salvation.

Arminianism

Arminians similarly affirm salvation by grace. The Five Articles of the Remonstrance state:

> That this grace of God is the beginning, continuance, and accomplishment of all good, even to the extent that the regenerate man himself, without this preceding or assisting, awakening, following, and co-operating grace, can neither think, will, nor do good, nor withstand any temptations to evil (Article IV)

Though Arminians emphasize human free will, they firmly teach that salvation is initiated and sustained by God's grace.

Salvation as a Process

Despite theological differences, all three traditions view salvation not merely as a momentary event but as an ongoing process involving justification, sanctification, and eventual glorification.

Roman Catholic Church

Catholic theology sees salvation as a journey. Initial justification occurs at baptism, but sanctification continues throughout life. The *Catechism of the Catholic Church* (CCC) explains:

> Justification establishes cooperation between God's grace and man's freedom. It is expressed by the assent of faith to the Word of God, which invites him to conversion, and in the cooperation of charity with the prompting of the Holy Spirit (CCC 1993).

The sacraments, especially the Eucharist and penance, are key to this ongoing process, sustaining the believer in grace.

Calvinism

Although Calvinists speak of justification as a one-time act, they also affirm that salvation involves a lifelong process of sanctification. John Calvin wrote:

> Christ justifies no one whom he does not also sanctify. These blessings are inseparable (*Institutes of the Christian Religion*, III.16.1).

The perseverance of the saints ensures that true believers will grow in holiness until the time of glorification, making salvation a process as well as an event.

Arminianism

Arminians likewise hold that salvation is dynamic. While initial justification is by grace through faith, the believer must continue in faith to remain in God's grace. Jacobus Arminius emphasized the necessity of perseverance:

> For no one is said to be in Christ, who does not continue in him (*Works of Arminius*, Vol. II, Disputation 11).

This process is not automatic but requires ongoing cooperation with God's grace.

Faith Alone Undermined?

Both Calvinists and Arminians claim to uphold "faith alone" (*sola fide*), but their emphasis on perseverance and good works brings them closer to Catholic theology than they may admit.

Calvinism: Faith and Perseverance

Calvinists argue that perseverance in faith and good works is the necessary evidence of salvation. However, this creates a practical tension. If assurance of salvation requires perseverance, the believer must evaluate their works to confirm their faith is genuine. In practice, this shifts the focus from faith alone to a faith-works dynamic akin to Catholic theology.

Arminianism: Conditional Security

Arminians teach that a believer can lose salvation through persistent unfaithfulness. This conditional security mirrors the Catholic idea that mortal sin can break one's state of grace. Both traditions require active cooperation with grace to retain God's salvation.

Catholic Parallels

Catholic theology openly affirms this relationship between faith and works, describing works as the fruit of grace. Where Protestants hesitate to admit a synergistic model of salvation, the Catholic Church explicitly teaches it:

> Moved by the Holy Spirit and by charity, we can then merit for ourselves and for others the graces needed for our sanctification, for the increase of grace and charity, and for the attainment of eternal life (CCC 2010).

This merit, however, is said to be wholly dependent on God's prior grace, aligning closely with Calvinist perseverance and Arminian conditionality.

The Real Culprit

The true point of tension between Roman Catholicism and Protestantism emerged with the Roman Catholic response to the Reformation: the Council of Trent. The specific canon that defined this divide is Canon 11 from the sixth session of the Council, which states:

> Whosoever shall say that men are justified by the mere imputation of Christ's righteousness, or by the mere remission of sins, exclusive of grace and charity which is shed abroad in their hearts by the Holy Spirit, and is inherent in them, or also, that the grace by which

we are justified is only the favor of God, let him be anathema.

This is the culprit. Protestantism, at least in principle, affirms that justification is by the sole imputation of Christ's righteousness. The Roman Catholic Church, however, rejects this, concluding—rightly (yes, rightly!)—that such a position implies that a person, once justified, could literally do anything and still remain saved. As I will shortly demonstrate, this is precisely what Free Grace theology correctly (yes, correctly!) teaches.

However, while Protestantism "technically" affirms justification as a one-time event based on the imputation of Christ's righteousness to the believer, the reality is more nuanced. Ask a random Protestant, evangelical or otherwise, and they will likely affirm that truth. Yet, upon closer examination, one finds that many hold a view consistent with what John Calvin wrote in response to Canon 11 of the sixth session of the Council of Trent:

> I wish the reader to understand that as often as we mention Faith alone in this question, we are not thinking of a dead faith, which worketh not by love, but holding faith to be the only cause of justification. (Galatians 5:6; Romans 3:22.) *It is therefore faith alone which justifies, and yet the faith which justifies is not alone*: just as it is the heat alone of the sun which warms the earth, and yet in the sun it is not alone, because it is constantly conjoined with light.[1]

Calvin's response, shaped by an erroneous interpretation of James inherited from Augustine and still pervasive among evangelicals today, essentially offers a non-answer to Canon 11. To assert that justification is by faith alone, but that justifying faith never exists without evidentiary works, is to tacitly affirm the Catholic position: "no one shall ever say that men are justified by the mere imputation of Christ's righteousness."

---

[1] John Calvin, *Acts of the Council of Trent with the Antidote*, ed. Henry Beveridge (Monergism Books LLC, 2024), e-book, 165.

Calvin, bound by his human limitations like many Christians throughout the ages and even today, could not bring himself to boldly proclaim the full truth of Scripture: that any justified believer, even if they fall into faithlessness, will never be abandoned by Christ. Christ's promise to His own remains unwavering.

Free Grace: A True Expression of *Sola Fide*

Free Grace theology represents a distinctive understanding of salvation that holds firmly to the principle of *sola fide*—salvation by faith alone. Unlike Catholic, Calvinist, or Arminian views, which involve conditions or evidence tied to perseverance or works, Free Grace insists that eternal salvation depends solely on a one-time act of faith in Jesus Christ, without any reference to ongoing sanctification or works.

Salvation by Grace Alone

Whilst all traditions affirm salvation by grace, Free Grace theology uniquely asserts that eternal life is granted the moment one places faith in Jesus Christ, without any conditions related to perseverance or fruit-bearing.

Catholic, Calvinist, and Arminian theologies often conflate justification and sanctification, suggesting that a lack of visible transformation calls salvation into question. Free Grace theology separates these doctrines, affirming that:

- Justification is a one-time event, entirely based on faith (cf. Eph 2:8-9).
- Sanctification is a separate, lifelong process of discipleship, which impacts rewards and fellowship with God but not eternal security.

Free Grace theologians point to verses like John 5:24:

> "He who hears My word and believes Him who sent Me has eternal life, and does not come into judgment, but has passed out of death into life."

This guarantees eternal life to the believer at the moment of faith, without requiring any subsequent proof or perseverance.

Salvation as a Moment, Not a Process

Free Grace theology rejects the notion that salvation is an ongoing process. It maintains that:

- Justification is a completed action with permanent results (John 10:28-29).
- Discipleship and sanctification, while desirable, are not automatic and do not affect the believer's secure position in Christ.

This contrasts sharply with:

- Catholicism, which ties eternal life to ongoing cooperation with grace.
- Calvinism, which requires perseverance as evidence of salvation.
- Arminianism, which holds that failure to persevere can result in loss of salvation.

Free Grace theology affirms that spiritual growth and good works, while encouraged, are not conditions for salvation. Faith does not look to its own performance, but to the performance of Christ.

Faith Alone in Its Purest Form

Catholic, Calvinist, and Arminian perspectives all introduce requirements or evidence that undermine the principle of grace alone through faith alone. Free Grace theology avoids this pitfall by teaching that:
- Works are entirely excluded from the salvation equation, even as evidence (Rom 4:5).
- Faith alone (*sola fide*) is sufficient for eternal life, as demonstrated by the thief on the cross (Luke 23:42-43).

This challenges the other main traditions:

- Catholicism explicitly ties justification to works (albeit through grace).
- Calvinism, by requiring perseverance as evidence, creates anxiety about salvation and risks making faith depend on observable performance.
- Arminianism, by making salvation conditional on continued faithfulness, places the burden of eternal security on human effort.

Free Grace theology critiques these approaches as compromising the sufficiency of Christ's finished work. Eternal salvation, according to Free Grace, rests solely on the promise of Jesus:

"He who believes in Me has everlasting life" (John 6:47).

Thus, Free Grace upholds *sola fide* in its most radical and biblical sense. By teaching that faith alone secures eternal life, Free Grace avoids the pitfalls of adding fallible conditions or insufficient evidence to justification. Unlike Catholicism, Calvinism, and Arminianism, it offers complete assurance of salvation, rooted in the promises of Christ rather than human performance.

Conclusion

Far from being sharply divided, the Catholic, Calvinist, and Arminian views on salvation share profound commonalities. All affirm that salvation is a gift of God's grace, see it as an ongoing process, and recognize the necessity of faith and good works. Ironically, despite their claims of *sola fide*, both Calvinists and Arminians introduce conditions related to perseverance, aligning them more closely with the Catholic emphasis on cooperation with grace. These shared elements should challenge evangelicals to reconsider the tendency to quickly label Catholics as non-Christians solely because of perceived works-based salvation.

Many across the Christian spectrum fail to differentiate between justification (a past event secured by faith alone), sanctification (a present process of spiritual growth), and glorification (a future promise of perfection). This conflation fallacy leads to viewing salvation as an ongoing process rather than recognizing that eternal life is a one-time gift received through faith in Christ.

Therefore, while we believe Catholic doctrine contains serious errors, so too do Arminianism and Calvinism. However, it is vital to distinguish between pseudo-Christian cults and those who affirm orthodox truths about Jesus: that he is the Christ, the Son of God, who died and rose again bodily for the salvation of those who believe in him. Unlike cults, the Roman Catholic Church holds to these foundational truths. If we desire to correct their doctrinal errors, we must begin from this shared foundation—just as we do when engaging with Arminians and Calvinists.

Can You Lose Your Salvation?[1]

Jon Tretsven

Introduction

When anyone believes in Jesus' name (John 1:12), they become a child of God and are "in Christ." The Holy Spirit baptizes them, in a permanent action, into the Body of Christ (1 Cor 12:13). Their salvation is secure for multiple reasons, any of which is sufficient to guarantee their eternal salvation. Louis Sperry Chafer identified thirty-three divine accomplishments that occur the moment someone believes in Jesus as his Savior. No one and nothing can undo these divine actions. Furthermore, if words have any meaning, eternal life means that a believer lives forever.

Here are more Bible promises you can rely on.

We Can Rely on God Our Father

Jesus said,

> "And I give eternal life to them, and they will never perish; and no one will snatch them out of My hand. My Father, who has given them to Me, is greater than all; and no one is able to snatch them out of the Father's hand" (John 10:28-29).

---

[1] Article adapted from Cuurio.com

Is an all-powerful God not able to save to the uttermost?

> "Behold, the *Lord's* hand is not so short that it cannot save" (Isa 59:1, emphasis added).

We Can Rely on Our Savior, Jesus Christ

He has perfected believers "for all time."

> **But He [Jesus], having offered one sacrifice for sins for all time,** *sat down at the right hand of God*....**For by one offering He has perfected for all time those who are sanctified** (Heb 10:12-14, emphasis added).

Sitting down signifies that Jesus' work as a sacrifice for sins has satisfied God's wrath against sin. The Old Covenant priests could never sit down—there wasn't even a chair in the temple! We can add nothing to Jesus' salvation; we simply receive His finished work on our behalf:

> **Jesus said to them, "I am the bread of life; he who comes to Me will not hunger, and he who believes in Me will never thirst...the one who comes to Me I will certainly not cast out...This is the will of Him who sent Me, that of all that He has given Me I lose nothing, but raise it up on the last day...that everyone who beholds the Son and believes in Him will have eternal life, and I Myself will raise him up on the last day"** (John 6:35-40).

In an *ou mē* statement—a double negative in the Greek—Jesus promised that everyone who comes to Him will never, no not ever, hunger or thirst.

In another *ou mē* statement, Jesus promised that He will never, no not ever, cast that person out.

Jesus assured believers that it's the Father's will that Jesus will lose none of those given to Him by the Father; instead, He will raise them on the last day.

Furthermore, Jesus declared that it's the Father's will for everyone who sees Jesus and believes in Him to have eternal life, and He emphasizes again, He will raise them on the last day.

We Can Rely on the Holy Spirit

> Do not grieve the Holy Spirit of God, by whom you were sealed for the day of redemption (Eph 4:30).

Can anything separate a believer from God's love? The Apostle Paul says no:

> For I am convinced that neither death, nor life, nor angels, nor principalities, nor things present, nor things to come, nor powers, nor height, nor depth, nor any other created thing, will be able to separate us from the love of God, which is in Christ Jesus our Lord (Rom 8:38-39).

We Can Rely on Jesus' Finished Work

What, you may ask, if we continue to sin after believing and having eternal life?

The Bible tells us we will continue to sin (1 John 1:8-9). For believers, sin impacts our temporal fellowship with God, but not our eternal life in Christ. Jesus paid for all our sins—past, present, and future. As stated in Heb 9:12,

> He [Jesus] entered the Most Holy Place once for all, having obtained eternal redemption.

While there are consequences for a believer's sins, including the possibility of physical death (1 Cor 11:30), none of these consequences is ever the loss of their salvation.

How to Know if You're Going to Heaven

> But when Christ appeared [as] a high priest of the good things to come, He entered through...

His own blood, He entered the holy place once for all, having obtained eternal redemption (Heb 9:11-12).

Because Jesus made it to heaven and God accepted Him, the Father will also accept those who believe in the Son:

> For Christ did not enter holy places made with hands, which are patterned after the true one, but into heaven itself, now to appear in the presence of God for us (Heb 9:24).

Focus on the Savior, Not Yourself

Since Jesus has secured eternal redemption, you don't add anything to His work. You simply rest in Him.

> Every priest stands daily ministering and offering time after time the same sacrifices, which can never take away sins; but He, having offered one sacrifice for sins for all time, *sat down at the right hand of God* (Heb 10:11-12, emphasis added).

Focus on God's Unbreakable Promise to Believers

The Scriptures say to believe in Jesus' name. The promise is that we possess, in the present tense, eternal life—we have it now! Words are meaningless if eternal doesn't mean forever.

> "For God so loved the world, that He gave His only begotten Son, that whoever believes in Him shall not perish, but have eternal life" (John 3:16).

Focus on Your Responsibility: Belief

You do not contribute to your salvation; instead, you believe in the salvation that Jesus provides. Faith in His name is the way you receive it. Each person is responsible before God to rest in what Jesus has done to secure their salvation. To do this, you must believe in Jesus' name; believe that He has completed your salvation by dying on the cross for your sins and resurrecting to life (1 Cor 15:1-8).

> But as many as received Him [Jesus], to them He gave the right to become children of God, even to those who believe His name, who were born, not of blood nor of the will of the flesh nor of the will of man, but of God" (John 1:12).

Don't Focus on Your Behavior

While you live on this earth, you will still commit sins. If you focus on yourself, you will know you aren't good enough for heaven. It's not about whether you're good enough; it's whether Jesus is good enough. He is your Savior, not you:

> If we say that we have not sinned, we make Him a liar and His word is not in us (1 John 1:10).

Don't Contribute Any Works

> Therefore they said to Him, "What shall we do, so that we may work the works of God?" Jesus answered and said to them, "This is the work of God, that you believe in Him whom He has sent" (John 6:29).

Have you believed in Jesus' name? If so, you can rely on God's promise that you will join him in heaven.

Have you believed in Jesus' name? Then you can trust God's promise that you have eternal life that you cannot lose.

A Response to "Whoever Believes" as Present Tense

Aaron Aquinas

"Because the sheep there are defined as those who follow Christ. The Greek present tense is used. They follow and continue to follow Christ. They believe in Him. It's the Greek present tense again. They believe and continue to believe in Him." ~Joe Schimmel

Introduction

This article argues that John 3:16 and its context do not teach a conditional or ongoing requirement of faith to maintain salvation but instead affirm that eternal life is a permanent possession given at the moment one believes.

Why does this matter? The belief that eternal life can be lost through lapses in faith creates fear, insecurity, and legalism. But if eternal life is truly a gift received by belief, not maintained by effort, then the believer can rest in the finished work of Christ. Assurance of salvation flows not from human persistence, but from God's unchanging promise.

A Key Verse

John 3:16 is arguably the most recognized verse in the New Testament. Because of this familiarity, it's also one of the most debated, particularly regarding the verb tense of "believes." Some argue that the present-tense participle of this verb implies a continual condition, i.e., that one must persist in belief to retain eternal life. According to this view, if someone ever stops believing (falling into apostasy), they forfeit eternal life.

John Wesley's theological influence starting in the 18th century is one of the most prominent impacting this perspective. A good summary of his thoughts around the present tense nature of faith is in his dialogue called "A Dialogue between an Antinomian and his Friend". He poses a question and answer::

> Question: "Can a child of God then go to hell? Or can a man be a child of God today, and a child of the devil tomorrow? If God is our Father once, is he not our Father always?"
>
> Answer: "A child of God, that is, a true believer, (for he that believeth is born of God,) while he continues a true believer, cannot go to hell. But, If a believer make shipwreck of the faith, he is no longer a child of God. And then he may go to hell, yea, and certainly will, if he continues in unbelief. If a believer may make shipwreck of the faith, then a man that believes now may be an unbeliever some time hence; yea, very possibly, tomorrow; but, if so, he who is a child of God today, may be a child of the devil tomorrow. For, God is the Father of them that believe, so long as they believe. But the devil is the father of them that believe not, whether they did once believe or no."[1]

But this interpretation, while popular in some circles, is both logically flawed and contradicted by the context of the very passage it attempts to cite.

The Self-Refuting Nature of the Argument

The argument relies on the fact that "believes" is present tense.

---

[1] John Wesley, "Serious Thoughts Upon Perseverance of the Saints." *The Works of John Wesley, Volume 1* (Grand Rapids, MI: Baker, 2007).

The conclusion drawn is that eternal life is conditional upon continual belief—a person must persist in faith until death to retain salvation. Following this logic, passages like John 3:16, 3:36, 5:24, and 6:47 could be reworded as: "Whoever continues believing (until death) has eternal life."

But here's the problem: the verb "has" as in "has eternal life" is also in the present tense. Suppose these passages require continuous belief for one to eventually obtain eternal life. In that case, logically, no living person today currently possesses eternal life because no living person today has yet met the condition of believing until the end.

This interpretation undermines its own use of the present tense. If belief must be ongoing, and the result (eternal life) is also present tense, then no living person could possess eternal life yet, a contradiction in terms. Furthermore, it makes the very idea of "losing salvation" incoherent: you cannot lose something you never had.

Answers in the Context of John 3

Beyond the logical refutation, the very context of John 3:16 answers this dilemma plainly and definitively.

> **"For God so loved the world, that he gave his only Son, that whoever believes in him should not perish but have eternal life."**

Here, "eternal life" is directly contrasted with "perishing." Belief results in one not perishing. That is, in receiving eternal life. This binary structure is continued in the verses that follow. Continuing in v 17:

> **"For God did not send his Son into the world to condemn the world, but in order that the world might be saved through him."**

Here, condemnation is the opposite of salvation. So "eternal life" (v 16) is equivalent to "salvation" (v 17), while "perishing" is equivalent to "condemnation."

The contrast Jesus presents is not between degrees of belief or the duration of belief, but between two fixed, mutually exclusive states:

perishing or not perishing, condemned or not condemned. These are not conditions that fluctuate with time or spiritual performance. The decisive factor is singular: belief. Importantly, the text says "whoever believes" in the present tense participle. The result it promises is *eternal life*, not *ongoing probation*. The very nature of "eternal life" implies an irreversible possession once granted. If belief were only effective so long as it was maintained, then "eternal life" would cease to be eternal. It would be provisional, contingent, and temporary. That interpretation would collapse the contrast Jesus is drawing and replace the clarity of His offer with ambiguity.

But the context resists that: Jesus is offering certainty. The dichotomy shows that belief transfers a person once and for all from perishing and condemnation to eternal life. Therefore, the contrast supports the conclusion that a single act of belief results in a permanent status of salvation and eternal life, rather than one that requires continuous effort or ongoing belief.

Born Again, Not Working Up to Life

Looking further back in the chapter, we see that Jesus introduces this entire discussion with Nicodemus by explaining the necessity of being "born again":

> "...unless one is born again he cannot see the kingdom of God" (John 3:3).

This same theme is echoed across the New Testament: we are not gradually justified through deeds or morality. We begin as spiritually dead and are born into life through Christ (Eph 2:1-5; Titus 3:5; 1 Pet 1:3). We are not children of God by default who risk being disowned. Instead, we begin outside of God's family and are adopted into it by grace through faith (Rom 8:15; Gal 4:4-7; John 1:12-13).

From Death to Life: A One-Time Transfer

Scripture uses consistent themes to describe salvation as a transition. From death to life, from wrath to peace, from condemnation to justification. Like in John 5:24:

> "... whoever hears my word and believes him who sent me has eternal life. He does not come into judgment, but has passed from death to life."

Note again the present tense of "has eternal life," and the perfect tense "has passed from death to life." This is not a process one enters and exits. It is a completed transition. Moreover, John 3:36 reinforces the same dichotomy:

> "Whoever believes in the Son has eternal life; whoever does not obey the Son shall not see life, but the wrath of God remains on him."

Here, "believes" results in life, while "does not obey" (a phrase in Greek often parallel to "does not believe") means that God's wrath remains, not newly applied, but already present on the person.

Here is a snapshot of this consistent theme of a transition from one state to the other, a permanent transfer:

- John 3:16-18: Condemnation vs. eternal Life
- John 5:24: Passed from death to life
- John 3:36: Wrath remains on the unbeliever
- Romans 8:15, Galatians 4:4-7: Adoption into God's family
- Ephesians 2:1-5: Dead in sin, made alive with Christ
- Titus 3:5: Saved by the washing of regeneration
- 1 Peter 1:3: Born again to a living hope

Condemnation is Only from Never Believing

> "Whoever believes in him is not condemned, but whoever does not believe is condemned already, because he has not believed in the name of the only Son of God" (John 3:18).

Why are the people condemned already? That is directly answered in the second half of the verse (v 18b): "Because he has not believed." This is in the perfect tense, which means the event that happened is completed (or in this case, not completed) to the past participle. This is always true of the condemned person. It's because they have *not* believed, which is what the scripture means in v 18a by "does not believe." The person who is condemned is someone for whom belief has never occurred.

Think of it this way: Can someone who has believed in the past be described as someone who has not believed? The answer is no. The condition for condemnation is having never believed, not ceasing to believe. And the condition for eternal life is having believed. If one has believed, then the judgment of condemnation no longer applies to them because it is no longer true that they "have not believed."

This understanding aligns perfectly with John 5:24, again:

> **"He does not come into judgment, but has passed from death to life."**

What we see from John 3, and particularly in vv 16 through 18, is not a call to continually earn or maintain salvation through uninterrupted belief. Instead, it is a description of two states: one under condemnation (having not believed), and one possessing eternal life (having believed). The present possession of eternal life is the result of a past act of faith, not a constant effort to maintain it.

To claim that eternal life depends on continuing belief is to undo the present-tense assurance that Christ gives. Moreover, it denies the very logic of the text, which clearly distinguishes between those who are condemned for never believing and those who are saved by having believed.

The plain grammar of the passage shows us that never believing is the sufficient condition for condemnation. The opposite of this perfect tense, described as the present participle "believes/believing", is "having once believed".

Conclusion

Taken together, these verses describe two fixed conditions:

- Those who *have believed* possess eternal life and will not face judgment.
- Those who *have not believed* remain under condemnation.

In short, John 3:16 and its surrounding context do not support the idea that salvation can be lost if faith ceases. Instead, they affirm that eternal life is a present possession granted to those who have believed, and it cannot be undone, because the condition of condemnation (never having believed) no longer applies.

Let the assurance of John 3:16 speak plainly: eternal life is not a future prize for the faithful. It is a present possession for the believer. Once you've believed, condemnation is forever off the table, and the life you have is eternal, not temporary, not probationary, but secured in the Son of God Himself.

You Are Saved "If" (Colossians 1:23)

NATE OTTO

Introduction

Are you certain that you will be saved? Most interpreters make such certainty impossible with the way they handle Col 1:23. Some say a believer can lose their salvation by not continuing in the faith. Others say that not continuing in the faith proves they were never saved in the first place. While theologically interesting, these views miss Paul's point altogether. His intent is far less deep, but far more profound.

Time Stamp

To understand *what* is going on, we first need to understand *when* is going on.

In English, the phrase "if you continue..." sounds like a future condition. However, that's not the best way of reading this.

The relationship between Greek tenses and time is complicated. The verb used here for "continue," in the present, active, indicative, can refer to something that happens in general or something that's happening right now. Without getting too deep in the weeds, Paul could be referring to their current continuing in the faith or whether they continue in the faith at all, irrespective of time. Either way, the focus here would not be on whether they will believe in the future. The question is *do* they believe?

Notice how the ESV translates a similar conditional clause containing a present, active, indicative in 1 Thess 3:8: "For now we live, if you are standing fast in the Lord." This doesn't refer to a future situation. He's encouraged by the fact that they *are* currently standing firm in the Lord.

It's important that we not automatically assume that the "continue" in Col 1:23 is a future condition to be met. Paul could very well be referring to something present, i.e., that they are continuing in the faith now.

The "If" and Provocative Language

Now, for the meat and potatoes. What is meant by the "if"? Does it introduce doubt about whether they will be finally saved?

Hardly.

Paul is using provocative language that gets the readers thinking about the gospel they should and do believe. Notice how this same "if indeed" is used in Eph 3:2. "For this reason I, Paul, a prisoner of Christ Jesus on behalf of you Gentiles—if indeed you have heard of the stewardship of God's grace that was given to me for you..." What is Paul doing with this "if indeed"?

Certainly, his apostleship is not contingent on whether they have heard about it. He's assuming, for the sake of argument, that they already understand his gospel ministry, and he wants them to comprehend it more fully. The HCSB effectively gets the point across by translating the "if" phrase as: "You have heard, haven't you?" The same thing is happening in Col 1:23. There's no doubt about whether they will be saved. He's assuming for the sake of argument that this is the faith they're continuing in.

Let me paraphrase our passage in Colossians to better make the point. "And you, who once were alienated and hostile in mind, doing evil deeds, he has now reconciled in his body of flesh by his death, in order to present you holy and blameless and above reproach before him, if of course this is the faith that you believe!" Paul is effectively saying, "You do believe this, right?" That's the point of the "if indeed." The Colossians are saved, assuming this is the faith they believe.

Why Use the "If"?

One could question, "If Paul isn't making their salvation conditional, why use the "if"? Why not just plainly state that they will be saved?"

Paul is using rhetoric to bring the readers in. Rather than just telling them they're saved—which he does elsewhere in Colossians (e.g., Col 1:13)—he draws them in so they come to that conclusion for themselves. Upon hearing this, they would think, "*If* I continue in this faith? Well, of course, I'm in this faith. Therefore, it really is true that I'm going to be presented holy before God. That's incredible!"[1] Other passages do this as well, such as 1 Cor 15:1-2. "...the gospel I preached to you, which you received, in which you stand, and by which you are being saved, if you hold fast to the word I preached to you—unless you believed in vain." They did hear it. They did receive it. They have taken their stand on it. They are also being saved by this gospel, if, of course, they do believe it! This type of rhetoric doesn't create a condition to be met. It assumes the condition is true for the sake of argument.

Putting the Pieces Together

"Continue in the faith" is likely describing a present reality (i.e. they are continuing in the faith). The question is not whether they *will* believe. The point is *do* they believe? The "if indeed" assumes that they do. The goal of Paul's rhetoric is for them to recognize that they will be saved because they're in the only faith that saves.

Rather than causing doubt about our future, this passage reminds us of the wonderful, secure salvation we already have. In Christ, sin is forgiven (Col 2:13). All believers have been raised with Christ through faith (Col 2:12). All believers will be with Christ in glory when He appears (Col 3:4). And this is true for you as well, if of course this is the gospel you believe!

---

[1] I've taken this idea of the reader's internal dialogue and even paraphrased the example from Daniel B. Wallace, *Greek Grammar Beyond the Basics: An Exegetical Syntax of the New Testament* (Grand Rapids, MI: Zondervan, 1996) 694).

Carnal Christians: No Such Thing?

GRANT HAWLEY

"The idea that you can be forgiven, reconciled, cleansed and now live an unrepentant, sinful life and somehow be a child of God is completely contrary to the whole testimony of Scripture and something that was unknown through much of church history."
~Michael Brown

Introduction

First Corinthians 3:1-4 is a passage that has ironically been a source of contention between Christians with different views. Lewis Sperry Chafer had a dictionary of theological cuss words and guilt-by-association arguments hurled at him for publishing his view that 1 Cor 2:14-3:4 does indeed teach the existence of carnal Christians. That 1 Corinthians was written to Christians is not in doubt (see 1:2, 26, 30; 3:16; 6:19-20). And even in the passage in question, Paul compares them to "babes in Christ" (3:1), which is a poor comparison if they are not *in Christ*. For this reason, the disagreement about this passage is not on whether these carnal people are truly Christians, but whether these Christians are rightly characterized as carnal in general.

For example, Brian Borgman writes from the Reformed perspective:

> Nevertheless, Paul does not imply that their carnality is universal, but rather localized to one serious and destructive area, their arrogant party-spirit. Paul is not

saying that they are completely carnal, he is pointing out that in this area they are acting like normal men (3:3b-4). He is telling them that they have the characteristics of the flesh. He then points out that this is the source of their jealousy and rivalry. In acting like this Paul could ask, "are you not being only too human?" (3:4b NJB).[1]

The Corinthians' Carnality

But was their carnality truly "localized to one serious and destructive area"? Or was their carnality indeed "the rule in their lives"? Sadly, it seems to be the latter. Of course, in the immediate context, Paul is addressing only their sectarian attitudes, "...for you are still carnal. For where there are envy, strife, and divisions among you, are you not carnal and behaving like mere men? For when one says, 'I am of Paul,' and another, 'I am of Apollos,' are you not carnal?" (1 Cor 3:3-4).

But the rest of 1 Corinthians was also written to the same people at the same time. These same brothers were tolerating, and even puffed up over, sexual sin within the congregation (1 Cor 5:1-8). One of them was sexually involved with his stepmother (1 Cor 5:1).[2] These

---

[1] Brian Borgman, "Rethinking a Much Abused Text: 1 Corinthians 3:1-15," *Reformation and Revival Journal* (Winter 2002), 79.

[2] The NASB rendering, "so-called brother" in 5:11 is troublesome because it implies that the brother is not really a brother. But this translation is not supported by the Greek text. The phrase in the Greek is, *tis adelphos onomazomenos*, literally, "anyone named a brother" as in the NKJV. In fact, nowhere in the New Testament or the Septuagint (the ancient Greek translation of the Old Testament) is *onomazō* used to imply that something is not genuine. This is reading modern jargon back into the New Testament. When this verse is put in context, it is even more obvious that a believer is intended. Paul wrote, "I wrote to you in my epistle not to keep company with sexually immoral people. Yet I certainly did not mean with the sexually immoral people of this world, or with the covetous, or extortioners, or idolaters, since then you would need to go out of the world. But now I have written to you not to keep company with anyone named a brother, who is sexually immoral, or covetous, or an idolater, or a reviler, or a drunkard, or an extortioner—not even to eat with such a person. For what have I to do with judging those also who are outside? Do you not judge those who are inside? But those who are outside God judges. Therefore 'put away from yourselves the evil person'" (1 Cor 5:9-13). They should not keep company with this immoral

brothers were suing one another in the unbelievers' courts (1 Cor 6:1-7). They were doing wrong and cheating their brothers (1 Cor 6:8). It is likely that they were involved in sexual immorality (1 Cor 6:12-20). They were fighting over food and wine and getting drunk at the Lord's Supper (1 Cor 11:17-22). They were lobbying for position and attention "you are zealously desiring the best gifts," (1 Cor 12:31, literal translation) and were taking their spiritual gifts as an opportunity to edify themselves rather than the church (cf. 1 Cor 12:7; 14:4; and Eph 4:11-16). All of these issues indicate that they were selfish and generally lived without love for one another. The famous "love chapter," 1 Corinthians 13, was not written to give pastors something to read at weddings; it was given to show these brothers a better way to live amongst each other. How can we look at the book as a whole and claim that these Corinthian Christians were living in anything but pervasive carnality?

And what do sectarian attitudes really say about their walk with Christ? Jesus wanted nothing more than for His disciples to "love one another" (John 13:34), and said it was by loving one another that others would know that they are His disciples (John 13:35). Likewise, John tells us that if we hate our brothers we are in darkness (1 John 2:9, 11), and that if we don't love our brother we are "not of God" (1 John 3:10).[3] And every bit of the fruit of the Spirit from Gal 5:22-23 shuts down sectarianism in its tracks. How can a community living in "love, joy, peace, longsuffering, kindness, goodness, faithfulness, gentleness and self-control" be sectarian in the way that these Corinthian believers were? It simply isn't possible to be generally spiritual and living divisively at the same time. In fact, in Galatians, Paul describes "hatred, contentions, jealousies, outbursts of wrath, selfish ambitions, dissensions, heresies" (Gal 5:20)—all the makings of party-spirit—as "the works of the flesh" (5:19).

---

person specifically because he is a brother. The entire passage loses its meaning if this person were not Christian brother.

[3] These verses are about fellowship with God, not about testing whether we are born again or not.

What Is a Carnal Christian?

We need to be careful not to redefine carnal to mean that they don't care at all about spiritual things. A carnal Christian may or may not care about spiritual things. That's simply not the point. A carnal Christian is a Christian who lives according to the flesh (carnal means "of flesh"). It is a Christian who is living like a mere man (1 Cor 3:4), as if he were not the temple of the Holy Spirit (1 Cor 6:19), as if Christ did not live in him (John 14:20; Gal 2:20), as if he had not died with Christ and been risen with Him (Rom 6:1-14).

A carnal Christian may very well care about spiritual things. We have clear examples of believers who did indeed care about spiritual things (even very much), who were still carnal. For example, in Romans 7, Paul describes himself as carnal while living as if under the law. He was struggling, living in the flesh (see especially vv 5, 14, 23); yet no one would say that he was not concerned for spiritual things. In fact, he desired very much to obey God's law (Rom 7:14-19), but while living under law (in the flesh, Rom 7:5, 14), he was unable to obey. He was living as a mere man, trying to live up to a supernatural standard. That is why he said, "For we know that the law is spiritual, but I am carnal, sold under sin" (Rom 7:14), and "For I know that in me (that is, in my flesh) nothing good dwells; for to will is present with me, but how to perform what is good I do not find" (7:18). It isn't that he didn't want to obey, but that while living as a mere man he didn't have the means.

Likewise, the Galatian Christians were warned against pursuing spiritual maturity in the flesh:

> **O foolish Galatians! Who has bewitched you that you should not obey the truth, before whose eyes Jesus Christ was clearly portrayed among you as crucified? This only I want to learn from you: Did you receive the Spirit by the works of the law, or by the hearing of faith? Are you so foolish? Having begun in the Spirit, are you now being made perfect [mature] by the flesh? (Gal 3:1-3).**

This passage, as clearly as any other, shows us that to live legalistically is to live fleshly (carnally).

Even the Corinthian Christians were concerned with spiritual things (1 Cor 1:4-9). This is clear from their repentant response to Paul's letter (2 Cor 7:2-12) and the fact that the tenor of 2 Corinthians showed that there was marked improvement since the writing of 1 Corinthians (pastoral care like that of Paul tends to have that effect). It is likely from 2 Cor 2:3-11 that the brother who was sexually involved with his stepmother even responded positively to church discipline. Yet at the time 1 Corinthians was written, carnality invaded seemingly every area of their life together.

Conclusion

Are there believers who, through tragic circumstances, neglect from spiritual leaders, and/or bad choices, become completely hardened and unresponsive to spiritual things? Experience suggests that there are (see also Solomon in 1 Kings 11). And we know that if there are any such people, they are eternally secure (John 6:39-40; Rom 11:29). But that simply isn't the point of the passages in the Bible about carnal Christians. These passages are about living "like mere men."

But being like mere men is far from who we are in Christ. We are called to a Divine standard (John 15:12) and given Divine enablement (John 14:12-14; 15:5). Sometimes it's easier to simply say "you must not really be a Christian" than to bear the burdens of our brothers who are living like mere men. But we are called to bear their burdens nonetheless (Gal 6:2).

Carnal Christians exist. And until we recognize that fact, we will never be able to offer the kind of pastoral care that Paul did toward the Corinthians. We will never be able to help carnal Christians lay carnality aside and walk worthy of their calling. But those who are themselves spiritual must correctly assess the situation and "restore such a one in a spirit of gentleness" (Gal 6:1). Our brothers in Christ—even the carnal ones—are worth it.

Is Grace a License to Sin?

Lucas Kitchen

"Once saved, always saved makes the wide way acceptable. We're Christianizing the wide way. We have cut the whole idea of transformed living, we've cut it off at the knees." ~John Oswalt

Introduction

Is teaching salvation by grace a license to sin? You've heard that claim before, I bet. Supposedly, grace is some kind of sin pass. The claim is that if we teach that grace is truly "free" (as OSAS emphasizes), then we will inadvertently encourage people to sin, as they will no longer have their feet dangling over hell.

While on the surface, this has attracted many people to Lordship Salvation (whether of the Calvinist or Arminian variety), the false implication that's hidden in this statement is dangerous. Why? It's exactly what a self-righteous person would say. (And yes, it's possible to be saved and become self-righteous.)

Do You Ever Outgrow Grace?

You didn't trust in yourself for your salvation, but it is possible to think that everything after your salvation is your responsibility.

I grew up with this mindset: You receive grace for salvation, then you work really hard to be good after grace has done its work. The idea seemed to be that there was no place for grace after I was saved. But that's not how it works. So when someone says, "Don't teach that grace is free because that would be a license to sin," I want your self-righteous alarm to start blaring. Why?

While grace *is* the method by which we receive our salvation, grace is also an ongoing need. Being saved is a one-time event, but our need for grace is not a once-and-done transaction. Please don't take my word for it. Take the word of God. Notice how each of these verses shows that grace is an ongoing need.

> **And He said to me, "My grace is sufficient for you, for My strength is made perfect in weakness" (2 Cor 12:9).**

> **Let us therefore come boldly to the throne of grace, that we may obtain mercy and find grace to help in time of need (Heb 4:16).**

> **But He gives more grace. Therefore He says: "God resists the proud, But gives grace to the humble" (Jas 4:6).**

Do you notice that in each of these verses, grace is not something that is only given to us in the past, at the initial point of salvation, but something that continues to be given regularly? It is dispensed in an ongoing manner. In our time of need. In our daily lives. In our weakness. To the humble. And that's a good thing!

The Grace-Rejecting Mindset

So, let's analyze the mindset of a person who argues that we should not teach that grace is free, because that would be a license to sin. By making such a claim, they are implying that *they* have somehow stopped sinning without the use of grace. They are implying they have no need for grace in their daily lives. Ridiculous!

Not embracing grace daily likely means that you will find yourself as a pride addict, and God will resist you. Remember, God resists the proud. Therefore, God will discipline you and me for such a mindset. I don't want to be in that situation. I want to embrace God's free grace.

So, is grace a license to sin?

Whether it is or not, it seems a lot healthier to focus on the fact that we all need his free grace, not just on the day of our salvation, but every single day.

Grace Is Not a License to Sin

Antonio da Rosa

"The major evangelical voices are saying, 'You're saved by grace alone. It doesn't really matter how you live.'" ~ John Oswalt

Introduction: Confronting the Misconception

Few doctrines are more misunderstood—or more frequently slandered—than the Biblical teaching of eternal security. Critics often object that the assurance of irrevocable salvation removes any incentive for holiness. They ask, "If salvation can't be lost, then what's to stop someone from living however they want?" This objection lies at the heart of many denials of eternal security, and it stems from a fundamental misunderstanding of what grace is and how it works.

The idea that grace is a "license to sin" reflects a deeply contractual mindset—one that views God as a strict employer and salvation as a conditional arrangement. But Scripture portrays the Christian life as something *far more relational*. Grace does not operate within a legal framework of probation—it functions within a family framework of permanence! It is in this context that Rom 8:15 declares, "you did not receive the spirit of bondage again to fear, but you received the Spirit of adoption by whom we cry out, 'Abba, Father.'" Grace makes us sons, not employees on trial.

Grace is not a loophole for lawlessness. It is the secure foundation of a permanent family relationship with God as Father. Within this bond, God lovingly disciplines His children (Heb 12:6), holds them accountable (Rom 14:12), and places before them the motivating hope of reward (Rev 3:21). But even more, He invites them into a life of deep personal fulfillment—discovering the purposes for which they were born of God—and experiencing the joy of walking in them (Eph 2:10; John 10:10).

Far from promoting sin, grace creates the only environment where holiness and human flourishing can grow together: one rooted in love, security, and purpose.

A Proper Understanding of Grace

Grace operates within a family dynamic. It is not permissiveness, nor is it legalism—it is the stable environment of a Father raising His children. Once we have been born into God's family, the question is not whether we remain in the family, but how the Father now relates to us as His own. And here, the comparison to good earthly parenting becomes especially helpful.

Honorable parents do not disown their children when they disobey. Toddlers can be wildly rebellious, but no loving father gives his child up for adoption when the child throws a tantrum or lashes out rebelliously. They discipline, train, correct, and remain faithful in love. The same is true of God: "For whom the Lord loves He chastens, and scourges every son whom He receives" (Heb 12:6). Discipline is proof of belonging, not rejection.

This is the framework grace creates: the security to grow, fail, repent, and be restored without fear of exile. It is not leniency or indulgence—it is stability. It is this relational safety that makes obedience possible.

Grace raises the bar not by threats or fear, but by rooting the child in love. That is what empowers maturity. That is what fosters holiness—not anxiety over being cast out, but confidence in remaining loved while being trained.

The Family Framework: Security, Not Permissiveness

Grace operates within a family dynamic. Like good parents, God gives life without requiring prior commitment to obedience. A father doesn't demand loyalty from his children before allowing them to be born. Likewise, God doesn't require it for salvation. The absence of commitment doesn't result in spiritual abortion. Life and child-identity are always gifts, never wages.

Likewise, honorable parents don't revoke their child's place in the family for disobedience. Toddlers are notoriously rebellious, yet no loving parent gives them up for adoption because of their defiance. Parents welcome children into their families by grace, fully aware they will fail—and yet they remain children. But this doesn't mean that they will always approve of their children's behavior! Romans 8:15–17 confirms that those who are children remain heirs of God, even in weakness.

Approval is not the same as acceptance. Although a *child* is always *accepted*, not all *behavior* is. Within this stable relationship, discipline naturally follows (see Prov 3:11–12). Even strong discipline does not nullify the relationship. In fact, it proves the relationship. Hebrews 12:6 says, "For whom the Lord loves He chastens, and scourges every son whom He receives." The child is not cast out—he is corrected. As seen in God's dealings with David's line (2 Sam 7:14–15), discipline never cancels love or belonging. God's discipline is never a sign of rejection; it is evidence of His love and fatherhood. He doesn't abandon the rebellious—He trains them.

That kind of security is not indulgence; it is relational stability. And as we will see, this is the necessary environment for obedience and holiness. A child cannot flourish in fear, but he can thrive in love and consistency. Grace provides that consistency. Grace does not lower the bar—it raises a child to reach it.

Not a License, but a Launchpad

Within the family dynamic, the objections to eternal security lose their footing entirely. Grace is not passive or permissive—it is a structured, intentional system of training rooted in security. Those who accuse grace of encouraging sin fail to see that grace is not the removal of all consequences, but the beginning of formation. It is God's chosen environment for producing responsibility, transformation, and maturity in His children. Rather than lowering expectations, grace secures the relationship and then raises the standard by empowering the child of God to live with purpose. It is not a license to remain idle—it is a launchpad from which a life of meaning, reward, and spiritual growth begins.

Unconditional Acceptance Without Unconditional Approval

As a Father, God accepts His children unconditionally, but that does not mean He approves of everything they do. Acceptance secures their place in the family while discipline shapes their conduct. Ephesians 1:6 says we are "accepted in the Beloved." This is not based on behavior. Acceptance is the result of our union with Christ. Yet 2 Cor 5:9 reminds us that we still aim to be "well pleasing to Him." God's love is not on trial, but our response still matters. Acceptance provides the immovable foundation from which God begins His work in us.

God Has a Job to Do

As the head of the household, God takes responsibility for nurturing His children toward purpose, fulfillment, and maturity. Scripture calls this *paidia*—child-training (Heb 12:5–11). It includes these key dynamics that bring a child into the fulfillment of their calling, personal satisfaction, and lasting joy—all the while glorifying the Father who raised them:

- Chastening: God does not overlook sin in His children. He disciplines them with real consequences, both temporal and eternal, out of love. This is accountability, but never abandonment. 1 Corinthians 11:32 shows that believers may be chastened so that they "may not be condemned with the world." Even illness or premature death (v 30) may occur in severe cases of rebellion, but not as acts of rejection. Sometimes a father's patience is expended and commensurate consequences are unleashed. Though the Father's hand may be firm, it is never cruel. He would never expel *His own children* into the Lake of Fire.
- Prospects of Reward: God sets powerful incentives before His children. He desires them to reach the full potential of their birthright: joy in the present and honor in the future alongside Christ. 2 Timothy 2:12 says, "If we endure, we shall also reign with Him." 1 Corinthians 3:14 adds, "If anyone's work which he has built on it endures, he will receive a reward." These promises stir godly ambition in the heart of a secure child. Grace

does not remove the race—it simply secures your entry in it.
- Resources for Growth: God equips each child with unique gifts and passions—and then supplies everything needed to develop them toward godliness and lasting fulfillment. 2 Peter 1:3 says His divine power "has given to us all things that pertain to life and godliness." God never expects fruit without first providing the means. He gives the Spirit (Gal 5:22–25), the Word (2 Tim 3:16–17), and spiritual gifts (Rom 12:6–8) to help His children grow into fullness.

Far from promoting sin, grace places the child in a structure of loving discipline and compelling purpose. It is a system designed not to excuse failure, but to raise up sons and daughters fit for glory. Grace doesn't erase responsibility. It places it safely inside a relationship that cannot be undone.

Grace Inspires Holiness, Not Sin

Obedience flows from the foundation of security. Knowing that you are in the family of God and that you don't have to perform in order to be there, in conjunction with the knowledge of chastening and the attainment of reward, encourages a life of holiness. The love of the Father that brought eternal security—and the opportunity to share in His glory—draws us to walk His path, which always leads to personal and enduring fulfillment. Holiness is not just about duty; it is the road to becoming who we were meant to be. Grace gives us the freedom to pursue that purpose with joy, not fear.

In addition to fulfillment, grace fosters a responsive love toward God that transforms the way we obey. 1 John 4:19 says, "We love Him because He first loved us." When we no longer feel the need to earn our place in God's family, love begins to shape our motives. Obedience becomes less about meeting demands and more about honoring the One who has already welcomed us. Grace creates a relationship where love can grow, and in that love, we learn to walk in His ways from the heart.

This isn't mere theory. Children who know they are unconditionally loved do not naturally become indifferent to their parents—they grow and thrive. Likewise, believers who rest in the assurance of their place in God's family are better positioned to pursue godliness, knowing failure leads to correction, not condemnation. 2 Corinthians 7:1 calls us to "cleanse ourselves... perfecting holiness in the fear of God"—not to remain in the family, but because we already are.

Shipwreck in this life and loss of reward in the next are strong deterrents to disobedience. Paul writes in 1 Cor 9:27 that he disciplines his body so he won't be "disqualified"—not from salvation, but from the prize. Grace does not remove accountability; it places it within a context of purpose, promise, and possibility.

Performance-based and threat-driven households often produce anxiety, insecurity, and rebellion. Children raised in such settings rarely reach their full potential. How hard it is for those who grow up in these homes to discover their true passions and purposes! Parents who withhold acceptance until standards are met wound their children deeply. And when love must be earned, love ceases to be love.

Grace is freedom to mature! It provides the secure environment in which a child of God can stretch, stumble, grow, and overcome. 1 Timothy 6:19 calls us to "lay hold on eternal life," the superlative expression of the new life in the present that will follow us into eternity. Grace opens that path. It offers not just survival, but significance! It provides not just security, but flourishing!

Eternal Security *is not* permission to disobey.

Those who reject eternal security depict God as a harsh parent—dangling heaven before His children like a prize that can never be held, while threatening them with hell if they falter. But no child can develop under such fear. Grace doesn't dangle—it delivers. And where love is settled, discipline becomes formative, and holiness takes root. Lasting obedience grows best in the soil of unshakable acceptance.

Conclusion: Grace is the Doorway to Fulfillment

Grace is not spiritual laxity—it is *paidia*, the loving child-training of a wise Father. It brings discipline, correction, and the opportunity to grow into the fullness of all God intended. Grace invites us into relationship and supplies the structure that shapes us into maturity. To call it a license to sin is not only wrong—it is absurd. Only grace provides the safety to grow, the purpose to strive, and the reward that makes the journey worth it. Holiness can flourish only where love is secure and the path is guided by grace.

The Rich Beggar

Marcia Hornok

Perhaps you have heard the story about the beggar who frequented the gates of a large estate, owned by the town's wealthiest man. Every few days, the rich man's son would give the beggar food or warm clothes. When the son stopped showing up, the beggar learned that he had died.

For many days, the beggar grieved until he thought of a way to commemorate the son. The beggar's one talent was his ability to sketch. He saved up his coins to buy some art paper and charcoal and sketched a crude but remarkable likeness of the rich man's son. He asked the gatekeeper of the estate to deliver it to the grieving father.

A year later, the father also died. Many art collectors and investors came to attend the estate sale. The beggar stood near the fringes to see if the wealthy man had valued and saved his sketch.

The auctioneer began by informing the crowd that the owner's will had two stipulations. One was that the charcoal sketch of his deceased son must be auctioned first. The crowd groaned, but the auctioneer shouted, "Who will start the bid on this drawing?" No one responded. "Do I hear one dollar?"

Someone yelled for the auctioneer to get to the valuable art, but the auctioneer persisted. Finally the beggar held up his hand, clutching a dollar bill.

"Going once, going twice…sold to the man for one dollar."

While the beggar went forward to collect his picture, the auctioneer announced, "This estate sale has now ended."

When the crowd's protests died down, he explained the second provision of the rich man's will: "Whoever gets the son, gets everything else."

The analogy to salvation is apparent. When any of us spiritual beggars receive the Rich Man's Son we receive the right to become God's child eternally. "As many as received Him [Jesus], to them He gave the right to become children of God, to those who believe in His name" (John 1:12).

Because the beggar wanted the son, he got all the riches of the estate. When we become God's child, we get everything else God has for those who belong to Him—forgiveness of sins, eternal life, the Holy Spirit, a reconciled relationship, power over sin through the life of Christ in us, and Heaven after we die, to name a few.

Not only that, but these things are ours forever. A child can never become unborn. A son may grow up to resent and reject his parents, but he cannot undo his DNA. He will always be their son.

For ten years, I taught Bible classes in care centers in Salt Lake City. After hearing the Gospel for several weeks, a senior named Louise said "Yes" when I asked her if she wanted to believe in Jesus alone as her Savior and accept His promise of eternal life. In every lesson after that, when I talked about Jesus' death and resurrection, her face would light up.

She was in the Memory Care Unit, so it did not surprise me that one day after the lesson, she seemed agitated and wanted to ask me a question. She poked her finger at her forehead several times and said, "Sometimes I don't…I can't…well, what if I forget what Jesus did for me?"

I said, "That might happen, Louise. You might forget Jesus, but will Jesus ever forget you?" I reached out and held her hand, palm up. I put my fingertips into her palm and closed her hand around them. "Louise, Jesus said in John 10 that He gives us eternal life, and we will never perish. He said nothing can ever snatch us out of His hand. He said that the Father is greater than all, and nothing is able to snatch us from the Father's hand." I told her that Jesus and God are holding her in their hand, so she does not need to try to hold on herself.

How do I know I have salvation that is eternal? Not because of something I did or felt, but because Jesus promised it. Trying to hold on to Him is futile, because He holds me. My belief (faith) in Jesus, not my behavior, makes me a rich beggar who is eternally secure.

Parents: Let the Doctrine of Eternal Security Bring You Peace

Summer Stevens

He was sitting on the steps, lying through his teeth.

I actually couldn't tell. Lying is such a big offense in our house that our five kids rarely do it anymore. When they tell me something, I tend to believe it.

But my husband looked at our 13-year-old son and pressed the issue. I suppose he understood the heart of a boy and the kinds of things that boys don't want to tell their parents. In truth, he'd been staying up really late, after we'd all said our goodnights, binge-watching a comedy TV show. That's why he'd been so tired in the mornings and why he'd missed several assignments at school.

The issue itself was minor, but what surprised me the most was that he'd lied to me. My son was a Christian, and he knew better than to hide what he was doing and then try to cover it up.

He caved under the accusation, confessed, apologized, and we dealt with it. Yes, he received a consequence, but, because we have a thorough understanding of eternal security, no, his sin didn't cause us prolonged anxiety or cause us to question the sincerity of his faith.

Christian parents will find that the doctrine of eternal security brings peace in the midst of difficult days and encourages them to adapt their parenting styles to be most effective.

I'm no stranger to anxiety. Sometimes it's an irritating hum in the pit of my stomach and other times it causes my mind to work and rework conversations, to-do lists, and what-if fears. For mothers, the most significant concern is the eternal destiny of our children.

God graciously led my husband and me toward the Free Grace movement right around the time we were married and started a family. All five of our children trusted in Jesus for eternal life at a young age. We rejoiced when our youngest became a Christian, knowing that the destination of the most precious people in the world to us was securely in heaven.

I know that each child understood—as best as they could at the time—the gospel message and received it by faith.

When issues arise, I don't wonder whether my kids are saved; instead, I'm able to focus on discipling my children. The concern becomes their heart, not their eternal home.

This is a drastic contrast. When bad attitudes or concerning behaviors arise, my husband and I can approach our children with love and grace for correction and restoration, knowing that our children possess the Holy Spirit. We can teach them about conviction and character; how to respond when temptation arises, and how to ask for forgiveness to restore fellowship.

If each big issue caused us to question whether or not our child was saved, we would not only be anxious, but we would also miss the opportunity for discipleship, focusing again and again on the basics of the gospel message.

You don't encourage someone who doesn't know Jesus to act more like Jesus. Without the Holy Spirit, this task is difficult and would likely result in legalism at best. No, first you introduce them to Jesus, and once they have begun a new life with God, then you walk with them in the process of getting to know Jesus. Depending on their level of submission to the Holy Spirit, this usually results in a noticeable life change. *Usually.*

One thing that separates Free Grace believers from non-free grace believers is our acknowledgment that sometimes a Christian's life doesn't exhibit a noticeable change to those around them. This is no different with our children.

What saves a person is their belief in Jesus' promise of eternal life, even for a moment. Entrance into the family of God, just like entrance into a worldly family, is irrevocable. If I had a baby that only lived one hour, that baby would still eternally be my child.

I can't comprehend the depths of the mercies of God, and I'm so thankful for that.

God uses the imagery of a family, especially a parent to a child, because we understand that that relationship cannot be altered. We may disown or break fellowship with our parents, but they never cease to be our parents.

Many parents lament over the spiritual condition of their adult children. *They were a Christian growing up, but I just don't know anymore...* The simplest solution is to ask the adult child. When you were away at summer camp that one year and came back to tell me you were a Christian, did you believe, at that moment, in Jesus alone for your salvation? Did you accept His offer of eternal life?

If they did, then you can direct your prayers in a more efficient way—that God would bring them back into fellowship with Him and back into the Christian community. If your child affirms that they never actually believed the gospel message, then you know to fervently pray for their eternal soul.

As Christian parents, we must make the most of every opportunity. We must clearly differentiate our parenting styles according to the current eternal state of our children: discipleship for those who are saved; evangelism toward those who are not.

Why Eternal Security Is Important to Me

Dominick Macelli

The doctrine of eternal security, often referred to as "once saved, always saved," says that once a person is saved, they cannot lose their salvation. Before looking at John 5:24, let me explain why eternal security matters to me.

I grew up with a basic knowledge of Jesus and the Bible. However, I don't remember anyone ever making the Gospel clear to me.

I knew I was living a very sinful life and asked God for help. I had an overwhelming conviction about my sin. I would open my Bible many nights, unsure where to begin, and when I couldn't understand it, I would eventually give up and close it. After a series of prayers over time, God answered. Ironically, a Pentecostal preacher from the neighborhood came to my home. He asked me a set of questions that I affirmed. We didn't discuss works or loss of salvation, although I did express to him that I wanted to change my life. I really did. But it became clear after he reviewed some Bible verses that if I believed in Jesus, I had eternal life.

I believed in that moment, and all the burdens of my sins fell off. I knew from that moment heaven was my home.

However, after that encounter, my family cautioned me about his Pentecostal beliefs, so I quickly fell away.

Not long after, I met a Baptist neighbor from across the street. She seemed really knowledgeable about the Bible. I went to her and her husband's church with a friend I met in high school. My friend started fooling around with a girl from that church, and it discouraged me.

I fell away again.

I prayed to the Lord, and I was given another encounter. I went to a small party, and this guy was reading the Bible in the kitchen to his friend, who was the host. I was amazed. I told him to keep reading, and so he did. I sobered up quickly. I told him to keep reading, and he seemed shocked! After I kept telling him to read, he asked if I wanted to go to a local restaurant for coffee and to keep reading. Of course, I said yes! I had him read until around 6 AM! I couldn't get enough of the Word of God! But then he got into the book of Revelation, which freaked me out, so I avoided him.

One day, the phone rang. This was before cell phones. I thought it was my other buddy, and I remember thinking, oh no... However, something on the inside of me said: "Call him out." I did. I asked, "How do I know if you're from a cult or not?" He said that was a fair question. "Come to my parents' Bible Study and see for yourself." I went—and loved it.

The church they were affiliated with had multiple satellite churches in the Chicagoland and Northwest Indiana areas. The head pastor is now the president of Moody Bible Institute. I attended that church for a while and started catching conversations where people questioned each other's salvation. People would say that our church is right, and that one is wrong, etc. I thought all churches were basically the same. Boy, was I wrong!

Now, this church affirmed eternal security with their lips, but they were also a "fruit inspector" type of church. They claimed to believe in salvation by faith apart from works, but then looked at works for proof of salvation! That negated their view of eternal security, because you could never really know if you were secure. This led me to read books about it, then online discussions. I came across a lot of Reformed Theology folks. I thought, well, maybe these are my people. However, over time, I questioned the doctrine of the "perseverance of the saints" (POTS). It didn't register right with me. Something was off. I was debating online and was looking for eternal security resources, and for the first time (that I remember), I came across a Free Grace ministry that articulated what my instincts were telling me about Reformed Theology. Prior to finding this FG ministry, I wrestled with POTS. It made me miserable because I did not know if I was one of the elect who would persevere. The only way I could combat those thoughts was to remind myself of my conversion testimony.

Thanks to that ministry, I finally realized that assurance comes from believing in Jesus' promise, not looking at my behavior. From that point on, having now understood assurance of salvation, God set a fire in me to ensure I share my views in the public space of ideas. Those who know me know I work relentlessly to see this happen. I have worked on fumes, day and night, but God—who began this journey—has sustained me through it all. I now have peace (as I did from the beginning). It's my heart's desire that others have that peace, too! In short—this is my story.

in their salvation.

Suicide Is My Story, Assurance Is My Song

Sarah Coleman

We had been married for about eight years and finally settled into that comfortable rhythm that only experienced couples can manage. It was Easter Sunday. After church, we had lunch at his parents' house before heading home for family nap time. The warm April sun was flowing through the double glass of the back porch doors. Our six-month-old daughter snoozed quietly in her bassinet as I curled up heavy-eyed next to my already sleeping husband. I remember the feelings that swirled around on that pleasantly average afternoon. Optimism, hope, and peace were what characterized the first half of the worst day of my life. Little did I know that seven hours later, I would become the widow of a suicidal husband and an unprepared single mother.

I still remember moments of that night vividly, my mother-in-law running to the door with small drops of blood on her shorts, phone in hand, frantically giving directions to Emergency Responders…cradling my daughter who had woken from all the noise…making a conscious decision to not go out to my husband as he lay lifeless next to our driveway already in the presence of Jesus…conversations with police and detectives recapping every moment of our day and every valley in my husband's fight with depression…making countless pots of coffee as much to busy myself as to keep us all awake…my parents arriving in the wee hours of the morning to offer comfort and support after driving for 4 hours ignoring speed limits so they could hold me in their arms as they had so many times in my childhood…crying as I embraced my pregnant sister the next morning after she and her husband arrived with their 2-year-old daughter.

By sunrise the next morning, there were no traces of the tragedy that had unfolded the night before. As the sun rose, friends arrived bringing breakfast and offering to step in and run my husband's business for as long as I needed them. It had been roughly 36 hours since I had slept, and when it was time to finally rest, I cried in my mother's arms as she lay next to me, praying for God to heal my broken heart. A few hours of rest and more people came to my aid. One came and offered his services as a director of a local funeral home. He took care of every detail involving my husband's cremation and memorial services, then drove four hours the following weekend with his wife and four-month-old daughter to oversee every detail of the service. In the days that followed, I was blessed by so many people, some I had only met a handful of times, some never at all, new friendships, and people who were there the day I was born. I will forever be grateful for the love and support they showed me in the days, weeks, and months that followed my husband's death.

Many people have asked me how I held it together, how I coped with such a tragic ordeal. My answer has always been this: assurance. From the moment I heard that gunshot, there was one idea that rang true.

Assurance

Blessed Assurance. I have assurance that my husband has had eternal life since he was a boy. I finally understood what Fanny Crosby must have meant when she wrote the words to that hymn back in 1873. I had a deeper understanding of those lyrics that night. I knew where my husband was. He was finally at peace in the presence of Jesus and oh, what a blessed feeling that is! Despite the fact that my husband had struggled with depression and his faith for years, I knew he had eternal life. As a child, he believed in Jesus for eternal life. Jesus made us this promise.

> **...he who believes in Me has everlasting life" (John 6:47).**

My husband received eternal life the moment he believed in Jesus for it. So, when he pulled that trigger on April 16, 2017, his life on this earth ended as he awoke to live eternally with Christ.

I can't tell you how reassuring that is, knowing I will see my husband again. The assurance of knowing that our daughter will be able to get to know her daddy in God's eternal kingdom if she, too, believes in Jesus for eternal life. This one promise has been my blanket of security. Martha, the sister of Mary and Lazarus, had assurance as well. In John 11, we read of Lazarus' death. Her brother, whom she loved, had died while Jesus was away. When Martha saw Jesus returning on the road she said to Him, "I know that he [Lazarus] will rise again in the resurrection at the last day." Martha had assurance. She knew that she would be reunited with her brother in eternity because they both believed in Jesus for everlasting life. Jesus responds to her in v 25 by saying, "I am the resurrection and the life. He who believes in Me, though he may die, he shall live. And whoever lives and believes in Me shall never die. Do you believe this?" When Jesus asked Martha that question, she unequivocally said yes. She had assurance. Do I believe Jesus' words to Martha? Yes! I believe in the promise of Jesus.

How amazing is it that on the day we celebrated Jesus' victory over death two years ago, my husband continued to live his life eternally in the presence of Jesus? So, the next question I'll ask is, do you have assurance? Do you believe in Jesus for eternal life? Then you have eternal life. I hope that after reading this article, you now have assurance of where you will spend eternity.

> Blessed assurance, Jesus is mine!
> O what a foretaste of glory divine!
> Heir of salvation, purchase of God,
> Born of His Spirit, washed in His blood."
> *-Fanny Cooper*

How Eternal Security Encourages Missionaries

ALLEN REA

"I grew up in an assembly which taught that I've accepted Christ and now I'm guaranteed for all eternity. And the danger of that is that you tend to relax." ~Zac Poonen

Introduction

The doctrine of eternal security is not merely "a Baptist doctrine."[1] It belongs to every born-again child of God. During my 14 years of pastoral ministry, the doctrine of eternal security held me close. And during my first term on the mission field (3.5 years), knowing I was permanently in the fold of the Great Shepherd comforted me deeply. "Once saved, always saved" is a practical truth that profoundly applies to missionaries.

Eternal Security Builds Trust in God's Promises

The people who support missionaries are many and varied. While we rely on the people of God to "send us on our way," we learn a distinct dependability on God as we find ourselves foreigners in a strange land. Those of us who have answered God's call to be a "light to the Gentiles" go forth in confidence of His faithfulness to His promises.

---

[1] Charles Stanley, *Eternal Security: Can You Be Sure?* (Nashville, TN: Thomas Nelson, 1990), 3.

If we can trust Him to secure our salvation eternally, then we can certainly trust Him to meet our needs wherever we serve.

Eternal Security Fuels Bold Evangelism

So many issues are at stake in the truth of eternal security, and evangelism is one of them. Our great privilege is to proclaim the Gospel to those who have never heard it. As we testify to the love of Jesus Christ, we can describe His love as never failing and unending. The wonderful thing about eternal life is that it is eternal!

Eternal Security Provides Certainty in Uncertainty

As our family went out in faith, burning our bridges and following God's call, we tend to hold Biblical certainties close because so much else is uncertain. There are always, at least in the back of my mind, a great many questions. Should we go back home? Why do I not understand more of the language yet? Will our children be able to thrive here?

Circumstances are uncertain. Everything from visas, finances, government tensions, and physical and mental health seems to hang on by a thread.

In times of uncertainty, the missionary (and every child of God) has this certainty: "If we are unfaithful, he remains faithful, for he cannot deny who he is" (2 Tim 2:13).[2] The great ministry of Jesus Christ promises us that though all in this world may be lost, our souls and their salvation are eternally safe in His hands.

Eternal Security Gives Peace in Peril

In a world of temporal peril, Jesus boldly proclaimed: "I give them eternal life, and they will never perish. No one can snatch them away from me, for my Father has given them to me, and he is more powerful than anyone else. No one can snatch them from the Father's hand. The Father and I are one" (John 10:28-30). I describe this to new believers in northern Thailand as "the grip of God." As the Word of God makes

---

[2] All Scripture quotations from the New Living Translation, copyright © 1996, 2004, 2015 by Tyndale House Foundation. All rights reserved.

clear, we believers find ourselves in the grip of Jesus as the hand of Father clasps the hand of Jesus. In this grip, we should have no place for worry, anxiety, or fear. As Paul writes to the Romans: "Since he did not spare even his own Son but gave him up for us all, won't he also give us everything else?" (Rom 8:32). The new believer, forsaking his idols, heritage, and spirit worship, rejoices to know that the Jesus that welcomes him will never cast Him out. The missionary rejoices alongside him, assuring him or her that every need we will ever have is met in Jesus Christ.

Eternal Security Promotes an Eternal Perspective

Eternal security gives us hope for the future. As with anyone working in the trenches of missions, we look forward to the fulfillment of Rev 7:9-10: "After this I saw a vast crowd, too great to count, from every nation and tribe and people and language, standing in front of the throne and before the Lamb..." We rejoice in the promise of harvest, as we see in Psalm 126: "Those who plant in tears will harvest with shouts of joy." We missionaries are, at best, "crooked patterns" for the dear people for whom we have sacrificed our lives for the Gospel.[3] The doctrine of eternal security beckons us to look for a new heavens and earth and solidifies our walk in the Spirit every day.

Conclusion

I am grateful for God's grace, which is shown in His promise of eternal security. This motivates me to continue preaching so that "Those who have never been told about him will see, and those who have never heard of him will understand" (Rom 15:21).

---

[3] Amy Carmichael, *God's Missionary.* (Fort Washington, PA: CLC, 1997),

Subject Index

Arminian 117, 119-121, 147
Arminianism 12, 18, 21, 115-117, 120-122
Arminius, Jacob 116
Assurance 5, 9, 22-24, 33, 96, 108, 110, 116, 121, 129, 134-135, 151, 155, 165, 167-169
Baptism 22, 34, 36, 115
Calvin, John 105, 113, 116, 118-119
Calvinism 8, 21, 114, 116, 120-122, 180
Calvinist 8, 117, 119-121, 147
Canon 114, 117-118
Charity 115, 117
Covenant 55, 57-58, 124
Creation 14, 67, 100
Discipleship 9, 17-18, 23-24, 88, 119-120, 160-161, 177-179
Election 8, 107, 109-110, 179
Eternal life 8, 10-11, 13, 15-16, 27, 45, 68, 70, 83, 87, 89, 91-92, 94, 117, 119-127, 129-135, 156, 158, 160-161, 163, 168-169, 172, 179
Eternal security 3, 5, 7-10, 12, 14-16, 18, 22, 31-38, 71, 91-93, 95-97, 99-100, 107, 111, 119, 121, 151, 153, 155-156, 159, 163-164, 171-173, 177
Evangelical 17, 25, 118, 151, 178
Faith 8-17, 21-24, 27, 31-37, 42, 46, 50-52, 59-62, 65, 73-74, 78, 83, 88, 99-100, 104, 113-122, 126, 129-132, 134-135, 137-139, 144, 158-160, 164, 168, 172, 178-179
Faith and works 9, 35, 117
Forgiveness .. 12, 16, 51, 57, 158, 160
Free Grace 1-3, 7-8, 14-18, 21-24, 33, 38, 114, 118-121, 148-149, 160, 164, 177-180

Free will 9, 115
Giving 42, 83, 167, 179
Gospel 7, 15-18, 23, 42-47, 52, 55, 62, 85-86, 95, 113, 138-139, 158, 160-161, 163, 172-173, 179
Grace 1-4, 7-8, 10-11, 13-18, 21-24, 27, 32-33, 36, 38, 47, 51, 55, 58-59, 64, 83, 88-89, 104, 113-121, 132, 138, 147-149, 151-156, 160, 164, 173, 177-180
Heaven 11, 13, 15, 25-29, 37, 42, 45, 48, 53, 73, 80, 83, 93, 99, 125-127, 156, 158, 160, 163
Hell 15, 23, 43, 45, 47-48, 53, 59, 64, 70, 74-75, 77-81, 83, 91, 130, 147, 156
Hermeneutics 37, 178
Holy Spirit 13, 23, 95-97, 99-102, 115, 117, 123, 125, 144, 158, 160
Justification 12, 17, 33, 35, 48, 59, 113-116, 118-121, 133
Kingdom of God 42, 113, 132
Messiah 47, 50, 57, 86
Monergism 115, 118
New Covenant 57
New Testament 25-26, 33, 50, 52-53, 69-70, 78, 84, 129, 132, 139, 142
Old Testament 31, 46, 52, 55, 75, 77, 80, 142
Perseverance 8, 14, 32-33, 35-36, 56, 107, 110, 114, 116-117, 119-121, 130, 164
Redemption 13, 21, 53, 95-97, 101-102, 125-126
Reformed 8, 113, 141, 164
Resurrection 12, 37, 46, 158, 169
Righteousness 11-12, 28, 45-46, 63-65, 85, 114, 117-118
Sacraments 75, 114, 116
Salvation 4, 7-18, 21-26, 29, 32-34, 38, 41-45, 48-53, 55-56, 59, 61-63, 65, 67, 69-71, 73-75, 77-81, 83-84, 86-89, 91-93, 95-97, 99-101, 107, 113-117, 119-126, 129, 131-132, 134-135, 137-139, 147-149, 151-152, 156, 158, 161, 163-165, 169, 172, 177, 179
Sanctification 9, 56, 64, 107, 115-117, 119-121
Scripture 10-11, 14, 18, 27, 68, 77, 89, 119, 132, 134, 141, 151, 154, 172
Sin 4, 9, 11-12, 15-16, 24, 27, 43, 45-46, 48, 56-58, 64-65, 67-71, 77, 86, 104-105, 117, 124-125, 133, 139, 142, 144, 147-149, 151-156, 158-159, 163
Support 42, 47, 95-96, 104, 135, 167-168, 171
Worship ... 24, 52, 58, 60-61, 173

Scripture Index

Old Testament

Genesis 1 .... 7, 10
Genesis 15:1 .... 28, 177
Genesis 19:1 .... 76, 177
Genesis 19:17 .... 76, 177
Genesis 32:3 .... 76, 177
Genesis 32:30 .... 76, 177
Genesis 32:31 .... 76, 177
Exodus 32:3 .... 92-93, 177
Exodus 32:32 .... 92, 177
1 Samuel 16:1 .... 100, 177
1 Samuel 16:14 .... 100, 177
1 Samuel 19:1 .... 76, 177
1 Samuel 19:11 .... 76, 177
2 Samuel 7:1 .... 153, 177
2 Samuel 7:14 .... 153, 177
1 Kings 1 145
1 Kings 11 145
1 Kings 19:1 .... 69, 177
1 Kings 19:10 .... 69, 177
Job 1 .... 78, 177
Job 3 .... 76-77, 177
Job 13 .... 78, 177
Job 13:1 .... 78, 177
Job 13:16 .... 78, 177
Job 33:2 .... 76-77, 177
Job 33:28 .... 76-77, 177
Psalm 1 173
Psalm 12 173
Psalm 30:3 .... 78, 177
Psalm 30:8 .... 76, 177
Psalm 31:7 .... 76, 177
Psalm 51:1 .... 100, 177
Psalm 51:10 .... 100, 177
Psalm 69:2 .... 92-93, 177
Psalm 69:2 93
Psalm 69:28 .... 92, 177
Psalm 71:3 .... 76, 177
Psalm 72:1 .... 76, 177
Psalm 72:13 .... 76, 177
Psalm 126 173
Psalm 130:3 .... 10, 177
Proverbs 3 182
Proverbs 3:1 .... 153, 177
Proverbs 3:11 .... 153, 177

Proverbs 10:2............79-80, 177
Proverbs 10:25..........79-80, 177
Proverbs 11:3................. 79, 178
Proverbs 11:31............... 79, 178
Proverbs 15:2.............78-79, 178
Proverbs 15:24...........78-79, 178
Proverbs 19:7................. 79, 178
Proverbs 26:1................. 64, 178
Proverbs 26:11............... 64, 178
Proverbs 28:2................. 79, 178
Proverbs 28:26............... 79, 178
Proverbs 29:2................. 79, 178
Proverbs 29:25............... 79, 178
Proverbs 31......................... 182
Isaiah 25:9...................... 78, 178
Isaiah 29:1...................... 52, 178
Isaiah 29:13.................... 52, 178
Isaiah 59:1.................... 124, 178
Jeremiah 4:1................... 78, 178
Jeremiah 4:14................. 78, 178
Jeremiah 31:3................. 48, 178
Jeremiah 31:6................. 76, 178
Jeremiah 31:34............... 48, 178
Jeremiah 39:1................. 75, 178
Jeremiah 39:18............... 75, 178
Jeremiah 46:1................. 75, 178
Jeremiah 48:6................. 76, 178
Ezekiel 11:1.................... 48, 178
Ezekiel 11:19.................. 48, 178
Daniel 7:1....................... 28, 178
Daniel 7:18..................... 28, 178
Daniel 9................................ 85
Daniel 12:1..................... 85, 178
Daniel 12:11................... 85, 178
Joel 2........................ 48, 78, 178
Joel 2:2........................... 48, 178
Joel 2:3........................... 78, 178
Joel 2:28......................... 48, 178
Joel 2:32......................... 78, 178
Amos 2............................ 77, 178
Amos 2:1......................... 77, 178
Amos 2:14....................... 77, 178
Amos 2:15....................... 77, 178
Habakkuk 2............................ 60
Habakkuk 3:1.................. 78, 178
Habakkuk 3:13................ 78, 178
Zechariah 13:9................ 86, 178

New Testament

Matthew 2.................... 4, 83-86
Matthew 2:2............................ 69
Matthew 2:20.......................... 69
Matthew 5:1............................ 26
Matthew 5:19.......................... 26
Matthew 6:1............................ 27
Matthew 6:2............................ 69
Matthew 6:20.......................... 69
Matthew 7:2.............................. 9
Matthew 7:24............................ 9
Matthew 8:1.......................... 100
Matthew 8:12........................ 100
Matthew 10:2.......................... 70
Matthew 10:3.......................... 28
Matthew 10:28........................ 70
Matthew 15:4.......................... 69
Matthew 18:1.......................... 51
Matthew 23:3.......................... 86
Matthew 23:39........................ 86
Matthew 24.................. 4, 83-86
Matthew 24:1............ 83-86, 178
Matthew 24:1.................... 4, 83
Matthew 24:2.......................... 84
Matthew 24:6........................ 178
Matthew 24:6.......................... 85
Matthew 24:8........................ 178
Matthew 24:8.......................... 85
Matthew 24:13.......... 83-85, 178
Matthew 24:13.................. 4, 83
Mark 5:2......................... 75, 178
Mark 5:23....................... 75, 178
Luke 8:3.......................... 75, 178

Luke 8:36 .... 75, 178
Luke 9:5........................... 51, 178
Luke 10:2 .... 93, 178
Luke 10:20 .... 93, 178
Luke 12:3 .... 27, 178
Luke 12:3 178
Luke 12:33 178
Luke 12:33 27
Luke 16:1 .... 28, 178
Luke 16:11 .... 28, 178
Luke 19:1 178
Luke 19:1 28
Luke 19:17 178
Luke 19:17 28
Luke 23:4 .... 120, 178
John 1:1 ..... 7, 10, 123, 127, 132, 158, 178, 180
John 1:1 28
John 1:1 .... 12, 178
John 1:8 .... 56, 178, 180
John 1:10 .... 127, 178, 180
John 1:12 10, 123, 127, 158, 178
John 1:12 28
John 1:16 .... 7, 178
John 1:29 .... 12, 178
John 2:2 .... 12, 178, 180
John 2:9 .... 143, 178, 180
John 3:1 ...... 10-11, 70, 126, 129, 131, 133, 135, 143, 178-180
John 3:3 ....132-133, 178-179
John 3:10 .... 143, 178, 180
John 3:14 .... 10, 178
John 3:16 .... 10, 70, 126, 129, 131, 135, 178
John 3:18 .... 11, 133, 179
John 3:36 .... 133, 179
John 4:1 ....24, 155, 179-180
John 4:19 ....24, 155, 179-180
John 5:1 ....51, 179-180
John 5:2 ....11, 119, 133-134, 163, 179

John 5:22 .... 11, 179
John 5:24 ......119, 133-134, 163, 179
John 6:2 .... 127, 179
John 6:3 .....12-13, 124, 145, 179
John 6:4 .... 121, 168, 179
John 6:29 .... 127, 179
John 6:37 .... 12, 179
John 6:39 .... 13, 179
John 6:47 .... 121, 168, 179
John 10:1 .... 152, 179
John 10:2 .... 13, 120, 123, 172, 179
John 10:10 .... 152, 179
John 12:2 .... 28, 179
John 12:26 .... 28, 179
John 13:3 .... 143, 179
John 13:34 .... 143, 179
John 13:35 .... 143, 179
John 14:1 .... 145, 179
John 14:2 .... 144, 179
John 14:20 .... 144, 179
John 15:1 .... 28, 179
John 15:1 .... 145, 179
John 15:6 .... 100, 179
John 15:12 .... 145, 179
John 15:14 .... 28, 179
John 15:14 179
Acts 4:4........................... 10, 179
Acts 10:4......................... 11, 179
Acts 10:42 .... 11, 179
Acts 13:3......................... 12, 179
Acts 14:1......................... 75, 179
Acts 14:19 .... 75, 179
Acts 16:3......................... 10, 179
Acts 16:31 .... 10, 179
Acts 17:3......................... 11, 179
Acts 17:31 .... 11, 179
Acts 27:2......................... 69, 179
Acts 27:22 .... 69, 179
Romans 1:1 45

Romans 1:2 .... 42, 45
Romans 1:15 45
Romans 1:16 45
Romans 1:24 45
Romans 1:28 42
Romans 3 .... 21, 118
Romans 3:2 179
Romans 3:2 .... 21, 118
Romans 3:22 179
Romans 3:22 118
Romans 3:24 179
Romans 3:24 21
Romans 4:1 101
Romans 4:3 10
Romans 4:4 83
Romans 4:5 120
Romans 4:11 101
Romans 5:1 .... 12, 104
Romans 5:2 .... 23, 109
Romans 5:9 46
Romans 6:1 23
Romans 6:2 .... 11, 27, 104
Romans 6:23 .... 11, 27, 104
Romans 7 .... 4, 103-105, 144
Romans 7:1 144
Romans 7:2 46
Romans 7:5 144
Romans 7:14 144
Romans 7:24 46
Romans 8 ... 4, 14, 107, 133, 153
Romans 8:1 .... 14, 46, 53, 108, 132, 151, 179
Romans 8:1 .... 133, 153
Romans 8:2 .... 107-109, 179
Romans 8:2 107-108
Romans 8:2 .... 4, 107
Romans 8:3 .... 14, 107-110, 125, 173
Romans 8:3 108
Romans 8:11 46
Romans 8:15 .... 132, 151, 179

Romans 8:15 .... 133, 153
Romans 8:18 108
Romans 8:23 108
Romans 8:25 107
Romans 8:25 108
Romans 8:28 107-108
Romans 8:29 107
Romans 8:32 .... 108, 173
Romans 8:33 .... 107, 109-110
Romans 8:33 108
Romans 8:34 108
Romans 8:37 108-109
Romans 8:39 108
Romans 9:3 47
Romans 9:30 47
Romans 10:1 47
Romans 10:9 11
Romans 11 .... 3, 45
Romans 11:2 .... 11, 47-48, 145
Romans 11:3 69
Romans 11:6 22
Romans 11:22 47
Romans 11:26 48
Romans 11:29 .... 11, 145
Romans 14:1 .... 24, 151
Romans 14:12 151
Romans 15:2 173
Romans 15:21 173
1 Corinthians 2 141
1 Corinthians 3 142
1 Corinthians 3 27
1 Corinthians 3 .. 11, 24, 53, 144, 179
1 Corinthians 3:1 .... 11, 24, 53, 179
1 Corinthians 3:1 154
1 Cor 3:1 27
1 Corinthians 3:4 144
1 Corinthians 3:14 179
1 Corinthians 3:14 154
1 Corinthians 5 .... 51, 142

1 Corinthians 5:1 142
1 Corinthians 6 143-144
1 Cor 6 28
1 Corinthians 6 143
1 Corinthians 6:1 143-144
1 Cor 6:2 28
1 Corinthians 6:8 143
1 Corinthians 6:19 144
1 Corinthians 8 42
1 Corinthians 8:1 42
1 Corinthians 8:6 42
1 Corinthians 9 28
1 Corinthians 9 ... 42-43, 52, 156, 179
1 Corinthians 9:1 42-43
1 Cor 9:2 28
1 Corinthians 9:2 ..... 42, 52, 156, 179
1 Corinthians 9:12 43
1 Corinthians 9:18 43
1 Corinthians 9:24 179
1 Corinthians 9:24 41
1 Cor 9:25 28
1 Corinthians 9:27 .... 52, 156
1 Corinthians 11 .... 51, 125, 143, 179
1 Corinthians 11:1 143
1 Corinthians 11:2 51
1 Corinthians 11:3 .... 125, 179
1 Corinthians 11:3 154
1 Corinthians 11:30 125
1 Corinthians 11:32 179
1 Corinthians 11:32 154
1 Corinthians 12 .... 123, 143
1 Corinthians 12:1 123
1 Corinthians 12:3 143
1 Corinthians 12:7 143
1 Corinthians 12:13 123
1 Corinthians 12:31 143
1 Corinthians 15 .... 127, 139
2 Corinthians 1:2 101
2 Corinthians 1:22 101
2 Corinthians 2 145
2 Corinthians 4 104
2 Corinthians 4:1 104
2 Corinthians 4:16 104
2 Corinthians 5 .... 24, 100, 154
2 Corinthians 5:1 .... 24, 100
2 Corinthians 5:9 154
2 Corinthians 5:10 24
2 Corinthians 5:17 100
2 Corinthians 7 .... 145, 179
2 Corinthians 7:1 179
2 Corinthians 7:1 156
2 Corinthians 12 148
2 Corinthians 12:9 148
Galatians 2 .... 23, 144
Galatians 2:2 .... 23, 144
Galatians 2:20 .... 23, 144
Galatians 3 .... 10, 144
Galatians 3:6 10
Galatians 4 132
Galatians 5 ... 100, 143, 155, 179
Galatians 5:2 .... 143, 155, 179
Galatians 5:2 182
Galatians 5:4 100
Galatians 5:6 179
Galatians 5:6 118
Galatians 5:20 143
Galatians 5:22 155
Galatians 6 145
Galatians 6:1 145
Galatians 6:2 145
Ephesians 1 ..... 11, 13, 95-96, 99, 101-102, 179
Ephesians 1:1 .... 11, 13, 95-96, 99, 101-102, 179
Ephesians 1:1 .... 4, 95, 99
Ephesians 1:4 99
Ephesians 1:6 179
Ephesians 1:6 154
Ephesians 1:13 .... 11, 99

Ephesians 1:14 101-102	Colossians 1:23 .... 137-138, 179
Ephesians 1:18 101	Colossians 1:23 .... 4, 137
Ephesians 2 27	Colossians 2 .... 12, 139
Ephesians 2 ... 10-11, 23, 59, 119, 132, 152, 179	Colossians 2:1 .... 12, 139
	Colossians 2:12 139
Ephesians 2:1 .... 23, 152	Colossians 2:13 .... 12, 139
Ephesians 2:8 .... 10, 179	Colossians 3 .... 100, 102, 139
Ephesians 2:8 27	Colossians 3:2 .... 100, 102
Ephesians 2:8 22	Colossians 3:4 139
Ephesians 2:9 11	Colossians 3:23 102
Ephesians 2:10 .... 23, 152	Colossians 3:24 100
Ephesians 3 .... 104, 138	1 Thessalonians 2 28
Ephesians 3:1 104	1 Thessalonians 2:1 28
Ephesians 3:2 138	1 Thessalonians 2:19 28
Ephesians 3:16 104	1 Thessalonians 3 137
Ephesians 4 .... 13, 53, 101-102, 125, 143	1 Thessalonians 3:8 137
	1 Timothy 1 51
Ephesians 4:1 143	1 Timothy 1:1 51
Ephesians 4:3 .... 13, 53, 101-102, 125	1 Timothy 6 179
	1 Timothy 6:1 179
Ephesians 4:30 .... 13, 53, 101-102, 125	1 Timothy 6:1 156
	1 Timothy 6:19 179
Ephesians 5 .... 100, 102	1 Timothy 6:19 156
Ephesians 5:5 .... 100, 102	2 Timothy 2 .... 14, 43, 53, 59, 172, 179
Philippians 1 13	
Philippians 1:6 13	2 Timothy 2 101
Philippians 2 69	2 Timothy 2:1 154
Philippians 2:2 69	2 Timothy 2:1 101
Philippians 3 28	2 Timothy 2:1 ...... 14, 43, 53, 59, 172, 179
Philippians 3 93	
Philippians 3:2 28	2 Timothy 2:12 154
Philippians 3:2 93	2 Timothy 2:12 .... 59, 179
Philippians 3:20 28	2 Timothy 2:13 .... 14, 53, 172
Philippians 3:20 93	2 Timothy 2:15 43
Philippians 3:21 28	2 Timothy 2:19 101
Colossians 1 ... 100, 137-139, 179	2 Timothy 3 .... 155, 179
Colossians 1:1 .... 100, 139	2 Timothy 3:1 155
Colossians 1:2 .... 137-138, 179	2 Timothy 3:8 42
Colossians 1:2 .... 4, 137	2 Timothy 3:8 179
Colossians 1:12 100	2 Timothy 3:16 155
Colossians 1:13 139	2 Timothy 4 28

2 Timothy 4:8 28
Titus 2:1 .... 23, 179
Titus 3:1 .... 52, 179
Titus 3:5 .... 132-133, 179
Titus 3:11 .... 52, 179
Hebrews 1 .... 12, 23, 50, 55, 57-60, 62, 124, 126, 151-152, 154, 179
Hebrews 1 93
Hebrews 2 50
Hebrews 2:9 50
Hebrews 3 50
Hebrews 3:1 50
Hebrews 3:12 50
Hebrews 3:14 50
Hebrews 4 .... 110, 148
Hebrews 4:1 .... 110, 148
Hebrews 4:11 110
Hebrews 4:16 148
Hebrews 5 49
Hebrews 5:1 49
Hebrews 6 .... 49, 179
Hebrews 6:4 179
Hebrews 6:4 .... 3, 49
Hebrews 9 125-126
Hebrews 9:1 125-126
Hebrews 9:2 126
Hebrews 9:12 125
Hebrews 9:24 126
Hebrews 10 .... 50, 55, 57-60, 62, 124, 126, 179
Hebrews 10:1 .... 57, 124, 126
Hebrews 10:2 .... 55, 57-58, 62, 179
Hebrews 10:2 .... 3, 55, 57
Hebrews 10:3 .... 50, 59-60
Hebrews 10:4 57
Hebrews 10:18 57
Hebrews 10:20 57
Hebrews 10:23 58
Hebrews 10:25 62
Hebrews 10:26 58
Hebrews 10:27 58
Hebrews 10:32 50
Hebrews 10:38 60
Hebrews 10:39 60
Hebrews 12 ...... 12, 23, 151-152, 154, 179
Hebrews 12 93
Hebrews 12:2 93
Hebrews 12:5 154
Hebrews 12:6 .... 151-152, 179
Hebrews 12:6 153
Hebrews 12:23 93
James 1 .... 9, 68, 74, 94, 179-180
James 1:1 28
James 1:1 .... 68, 94, 179-180
James 1:2 77
James 1:2 .... 9, 74, 180
James 1:12 .... 94, 180
James 1:12 28
James 1:15 68
James 1:21 77
James 1:21 .... 74, 180
James 1:22 9
James 2 .... 73-74, 81, 180
James 2:1 80
James 2:1 .... 73-74, 81, 180
James 2:14 80
James 2:14 .... 73-74, 81, 180
James 4 .... 74, 148
James 4:1 74
James 4:6 148
James 4:12 74
James 5 .... 51, 68, 70-71, 74, 180
James 5:1 .... 3, 67
James 5:1 .51, 68, 70-71, 74, 180
James 5 68
James 5:1 68
James 5:2 74
James 5:15 74
James 5:20 74

1 Peter 2	28
1 Peter 2:9	28
1 Peter 5	28
1 Peter 5:4	28
1 Peter 1:3	132, 180
1 Peter 1:3	133
1 Peter 5	24
1 Peter 5:1	24
1 Peter 5:10	24
2 Peter 1	9, 110, 180
2 Peter 1:1	110
2 Peter 1:3	180
2 Peter 1:3	155
2 Peter 1:10	110
2 Peter 2	180
2 Peter 2:2	180
2 Peter 2:2	3, 63
1 John 1:1	127, 180
1 John 1:8	56, 180
1 John 1:10	127, 180
1 John 2:2	12, 180
1 John 2:9	143, 180
1 John 3:1	143, 180
1 John 3:10	143, 180
1 John 4:1	24, 155, 180
1 John 4:19	24, 155, 180
1 John 5:1	51, 180
Revelation 1	88, 94, 180
Revelation 2	28-29
Revelation 2	91-94
Revelation 2:1	94
Revelation 2:1	29
Revelation 2:2	28
Revelation 2:10	94
Revelation 2:7	28
Revelation 2:17	29
Revelation 2:26	28
Revelation 3	28-29
Revelation 3	28, 87, 89,

Contributing Authors

Charles C. Bing (BA, Washington Bible College; ThM, PhD, Dallas Theological Seminary) served in pastoral ministry for twenty-five years, teaches adjunct at several Bible schools, and is the founder of GraceLife Ministries (gracelife.org). His books include *Simply by Grace: An Introduction to God's Life-Changing Gift* and *Grace, Salvation, & Discipleship: How to Understand Some Difficult Passages*.

Lavern Brown (BA, Christian Heritage College; ThM, Dallas Theological Seminary; DMin, Western Seminary) served in pastoral ministry for fifteen years, has taught as adjunct at Southwestern Bible College and Phoenix Seminary, and is a co-founder of Advanced Pastoral Network (advancedpastoralnetwork.com). He is co-author of *Pastor Unique: Becoming a Turnaround Leader* and author of *Lifeless to New Life: Biblical Prayers to Resurrect the Lifeless Church*, in addition to numerous journal and magazine articles.

Marty A. Cauley (BS, Western Carolina University; MDiv, Southeastern Baptist Seminary) served in pastoral ministry for several years, followed by a career in the software industry. His ministry focuses on eternal security and eternal rewards (misthology.org). His thirty books include a two-volume magnum opus, *The Outer Darkness*. His series, *Misthological Models*, focuses on competing models of biblical rewards (misthos).

Sarah Coleman (BA, East Texas Baptist) remarried and lives with her husband Ben and their daughter Charley in Longview, TX, where she volunteers with Free Grace International and The Pines Church.

Antonio G. da Rosa (BABS, M.Div., Southern California Seminary) has served as both pastor and missionary, and has written hundreds of articles from a Free Grace perspective. He is currently founding an FG missions organization.

Daniel Goepfrich (BA, Faith Baptist Bible College; ThM, Tyndale Theological Seminary; DMin, Trinity Graduate School of Apologetics and Theology) has served as a Teaching Pastor for more than twenty years and teaches Bible, theology, and the biblical languages as an adjunct at several Bible schools. He is the founder of Theology is for Everyone (theologyisforeveryone.com). His books include *Hermeneutics for Everyone: A Practical Guide for Reading and Studying Your Bible*; *Biblical Discipleship: The Path for Helping People Follow Jesus*; and a three-volume *Chapter by Chapter* study covering the entire Bible.

Eli Haitov (BA, Israel College of the Bible; MA, Biola) is a lecturer and a PhD student (in philosophy). He has published several papers in peer-reviewed philosophy journals and has a forthcoming paper in the *Journal of the Evangelical Theological Society*.

Marcia Hornok (BA Washington Bible College) is the wife of retired pastor Ken, who served Midvalley Bible Church in Salt Lake City for 39 years. They raised 6 children and now enjoy 15 grands. Her books include *Fruit of the Spirit: Inspiration for Women from Galatians 5:22-23* and *Proverbs 31 Virtue Not Exhaustion*. She blogs at christiangals.blogspot.com.

Lucas Kitchen (BS, LeTourneau; MA, Liberty) is the Executive Director of Free Grace International (freegrace.in), and ministers at The Pines Church in Longview, TX. His many books include *Missionary to Mars*, *Naked Grace*, and *Eternal Clarity: Erase the Gray Between Believe and Obey*.

Valtteri Lahti is a Free Grace Christian from Finland with a strong interest in church history, particularly the historical developments of Free Grace theology.

Shawn Lazar (BTh, McGill; MA, Free University Amsterdam; DPT, McMaster Divinity College) is the pastor of Gateway United Baptist Church in Denton, TX, and a writer for Free Grace International (freegrace.in). His publications include *Chosen to Serve: Why Divine Election Is to Service Not Eternal Life*, *The Five Points of Free Grace*, and *The Myth of Tithing and the Joy of Grace Giving*.

Dominick Macelli founded Grace Answers (a digital website that features Grace Chat Ai) to equip others to distinguish salvation from discipleship and to magnify the simplicity of the gospel. He lives in Northwest Indiana with his wife, Mariaelena, of twelve years.

Kenneth McClure (BA, University of Alabama; MPPM with a concentration in international marketing, Birmingham-Southern College) is a teaching elder at McCalla Bible Church and works as a volunteer chaplain at a hospice organization. He is a retired business owner.

Jeremy Mikkelsen (AA, Ethnos360 Bible Institute; BS, Oregon State; MA, Chafer) serves as the Executive Director of the Free Grace Alliance. He has previously served as a missionary overseas and pastored two churches, including Lacey Bible Church, which he and his wife, Carri, helped revitalize.

Chris Morrison (BA, MA, Luther Rice; MDiv, Liberty) has served as a pastor, chaplain, and teacher. He is completing a PhD in organizational leadership at Southeastern University.

Luke Morrison (BS, Moody; MDiv, ThM, Liberty) has served in pastoral ministry for several years. He is the founding pastor of Archer County Cowboy Church.

Tim Nichols (BS, Southeastern Bible; ThM, Chafer) is a teacher, bodyworker, and pastor serving in Englewood, Co. His writing includes *Dead Man's Faith*, *Go For the Heart: Biblical Tools for Devotional Apologetics*, the Victorious Bible curriculum, and other works for Headwaters Christian Resources (headwatersresources.org).

Nate Otto (BA, Frontier School of the Bible) is working towards a MA in Biblical Exegesis, Cornerstone Theological Seminary. He has written several articles on difficult Bible passages and fills pulpit at a rural church.

Allen Rea (BA, Brewton-Parker; MDiv, DMin, Luther Rice) served as a pastor for many years and is now a missionary serving in Thailand with OMF International.

Vincenzo Russo (MSc, Federico II University of Naples; DipHE, University of Chester) has a background in computer science and theology, and is currently completing an MA in Theology at the University of Chester, England. He is the co-founder of *Gratia Gratis* ministries in Italy (https://gratia.gratis), which is dedicated to preaching, teaching, writing, and translating theological and pastoral resources rooted in the message of God's Free Grace.

Summer Stevens (BS, Western Oregon University; MABS, Dallas Theological Seminary) is a pastor's wife and mother of five children. She writes women's Bible studies, speaks at women's events, and volunteers at her church in the Outer Banks of North Carolina.

Jon Tretsven (BS, Dallas Bible College, Double Major in Biblical Studies), curriculum writer for BEEWorld 2003-2018, curriculum and writer for iTEE Global Missions 2018-current. Bible Content writer for Cuurio.com 2021-current.

Daniel J. Weierbach (BA, MTS, Liberty) is the Associate Pastor of Open Door Baptist Church in Prattville, Alabama, and the founder of the Contending 4 Christ (C4C) Apologetics ministry. He developed the Free Grace soteriological acronym LOTUS as a direct response to Calvinism's TULIP, offering an alternative theological framework. His well-known book, *LOTUS: A Free Grace Response to TULIP*, explores this in depth.

Shawn Willson (BA, Bob Jones University; MDiv, Capital Bible Seminary) serves as the pastor of Grace Community Bible Church in River Ridge, LA. He is married to his best friend Jennifer, and they enjoy raising their four children to God's glory. He also reviews books at youtube.com/revreads.

Free Grace International creates resources—videos, blogs, books, and tracts—to help people understand the beauty of God's free offer of salvation through faith in Jesus Christ. Too often that message is muddled by the idea that salvation requires a transformed life or a record of good works. We exist to bring clarity by distinguishing the free gift of salvation from the call to discipleship.

Check Out Our Other Books

John Goodding, *Not So Famous Amos*
John Goodding and Lucas Kitchen, *Evan Wants To Go To Heaven*
Lucas Kitchen, *Eternal Clarity*
Lucas Kitchen, *Eternal Life: Believe to Be Alive*
Lucas Kitchen, *Eternal Rewards: It Will Pay to Obey*
Lucas Kitchen, *For the Sake of the King*
Lucas Kitchen, *In Pursuit of Fruit*
Lucas Kitchen, *Missionary to Mars*
Lucas Kitchen, *Naked Grace*
Lucas Kitchen, *Salvation and Discipleship*
Lucas Kitchen, *Things Above*
Lucas Kitchen, *Thomas: Hero of the Faith*
Shawn Lazar, *The Five Points of Free Grace*
Shawn Lazar, *The Myth of Tithing and the Joy of Grace Giving*

Visit www.freegrace.in

www.ingramcontent.com/pod-product-compliance
Lightning Source LLC
Chambersburg PA
CBHW071339190426
43193CB00042B/1899